YORK NOTES

MUCH ADO ABOUT NOTHING

WILLIAM SHAKESPEARE

NOTES BY ROSS STUART

Longman

EG33222

York Press

822.33

M ᴜc

Exterior picture of the Globe Theatre reproduced by permission of the
Raymond Mander and Joe Mitchenson Theatre Collection
Reconstruction of the Globe Theatre interior reprinted from Hodges;
'The Globe Restored' (1968) by permission of Oxford University Press

The right of Ross Stuart to be identified as Author
of this Work has been asserted by him in accordance with the
Copyright, Designs and Patents Act 1988

YORK PRESS
322 Old Brompton Road, London SW5 9JH

PEARSON EDUCATION LIMITED
Edinburgh Gate, Harlow,
Essex CM20 2JE, United Kingdom
Associated companies, branches and representatives throughout the world

© Librairie du Liban *Publishers* 1998, 2004

First published 1998
This new and fully revised edition first published 2004
Third impression 2005

10 9 8 7 6 5 4 3

ISBN-10: 0-582-82303-X
ISBN-13: 978-0-582-82303-7

Designed by Michelle Cannatella
Typeset by Land & Unwin (Data Sciences), Bugbrooke, Northamptonshire
Produced by Pearson Education Asia Limited, Hong Kong

CONTENTS

PART FOUR
CRITICAL HISTORY

PART FIVE
BACKGROUND

PART ONE

INTRODUCTION

HOW TO STUDY A PLAY

Studying on your own requires self-discipline and a carefully thought-out work plan in order to be effective.

- Drama is a special kind of writing (the technical term is 'genre') because it needs a performance in the theatre to arrive at a full interpretation of its meaning. Try to imagine that you are a member of the audience when reading the play. Think about how it could be presented on the stage, not just about the words on the page.

- Drama is always about conflict of some sort (which may be below the surface). Identify the conflicts in the play and you will be close to identifying the large ideas or themes which bind all the parts together.

- Make careful notes on themes, character, plot and any subplots of the play.

- Why do you like or dislike the characters in the play? How do your feelings towards them develop and change?

- Playwrights find non-realistic ways of allowing an audience to see into the minds and motives of their characters, for example, **soliloquy**, aside or music. Consider how such dramatic devices are used in the play you are studying.

- Think of the playwright writing the play. Why were these particular arrangements of events, characters and speeches chosen?

- Cite exact sources for all quotations, whether from the text itself or from critical commentaries. Wherever possible find your own examples from the play to back up your opinions.

- Where appropriate, comment in detail on the language of the passage you have quoted.

- Always express your ideas in your own words.

These York Notes offer an introduction to *Much Ado About Nothing* and cannot substitute for close reading of the text and the study of secondary sources.

> **CONTEXT**
>
> 'Genre' is a type or category of literature, defined by common features or purpose. Drama, for example, is a distinct genre, because it requires staging. Within drama are many sub-genres such as 'kitchen-sink' drama (realistic British drama of the 1950s onwards) or tragedy or comedy, for example.

READING *MUCH ADO ABOUT NOTHING*

A 'merry war' (I.1.45) between two would-be lovers, dastardly plots, deception upon deception to thwart an arranged marriage, a dazzling masked ball, and Constable Dogberry's hilarious ramblings have all made this comedy enduringly popular, and time after time its revivals on the London stage have won acclaim. As early as 1640 a verse eulogy affirmed that the 'cockpit, galleries, boxes, all [were] full' whenever it was staged, and ascribed its popularity, as did Charles I – in his copy of the first folio – not to the romance between Claudio and Hero but to the 'merry war' of wit between Beatrice and Benedick.

It is possible to find parallels for *Much Ado about Nothing*'s courtly wit in *Love's Labour's Lost* and softening of the man-hating spinster in *The Taming of the Shrew*, both earlier works.

Of the mature comedies, *Much Ado About Nothing* is the most urbane and sardonic, and the least pastoral and romantic. That the play is dominated by warring rather than romantic lovers whose relations determine the course of the main plot has led some critics to question whether it should be called a comedy at all, but rather a problem play of obscure intent.

In *Much Ado* it is not a jester who **satirises** romantic love or questions social conventions. Rather, Beatrice and Benedick are the critics, and their realism is justified when Claudio breaks his engagement to his adored Hero. Their outspoken individuality enables them to stand aside to criticise society and themselves. In comedies such as *As You Like It* male disguise liberates the female characters from social constraints. Beatrice, however, wears no disguise, but combines masculine assertiveness with feminine coyness. Her union with Benedick is not a surrender to the moral and social conventions of Messina but a triumph of individuality. It raises questions about romantic love, the role of women and the male code of honour.

CONTEXT

Having a male actor play Beatrice, Shakespeare's most masculine comic heroine, would have added to the comic **irony** for an Elizabethan audience.

The play's title suggests that it is an entertaining trifle. It is deliberately frivolous. The attraction and therapeutic function of such comedy is as a diversion from the serious business of life. The 'ado' is the fuss caused by Claudio's rejection of Hero for nothing, a misconception, Don John's slander, which is so transparent that even the Watch stumble upon the truth and bring the perpetrators to book. The title also has sexual connotations, since 'nothing' was an Elizabethan **euphemism** for 'female genitalia', the 'ado' the perturbation caused to the male characters in its pursuit. In Shakespeare's time 'nothing' and 'noting' had the same pronunciation. Claudio asks Benedick in the first scene whether he has 'noted' Hero, the daughter of Leonato. From that point it is remarkable how much of the play is concerned with noting, spying, observing, eavesdropping, overhearing and misconceiving. Claudio falls into and out of love on appearances and Beatrice and Benedick, whilst they are eavesdropping on or noting their friends, are prompted by false report to fall in love with each other. This raises the issue of appearance and reality: how can true love be found if it is inevitably based upon illusion?

Beatrice's and Benedick's feelings for each other are not illusory. Their witty antagonism betrays a deeper attraction and affinity. Unlike Claudio and Hero, they fall in love against their declared mutual antipathy and antagonism to marriage: 'I had rather hear my dog bark at a crow than a man swear he loves me' (I.1.123–4). If they are opponents of the *status quo* and their relationship is endorsed, criticism of Claudio's and Hero's relationship is implied. While courted by Claudio, Hero is silent. He announces himself a most conventional lover expediently looking for a suitable wife after a war. Attracted by Hero's appearance, he courts her and her large dowry. He casts her off upon hearsay, seems untouched by remorse when she is reported dead and is rewarded with her as a wife when he repents. Shakespeare's intentions in creating a romantic hero who behaves so unsympathetically pose problems for critics, actors and directors. Though constantly popular with audiences, *Much Ado* has not won universal critical acclaim. Victorian critics condemned Beatrice as coarse and disagreeable, and Benedick as a shallow poseur.

 **QUESTION**

Are Beatrice and Benedick attracted to each other as opposites?

PART TWO

THE TEXT

A NOTE ON THE TEXT

The most authoritative text of Much Ado About Nothing *is the quarto of 1600. There are several excellent editions of the text available, including* The New Penguin Shakespeare, *edited by R.A. Foakes,* The Arden Shakespeare, *edited by A.R. Humphreys. The text used to compile these Notes is that used in* The New Cambridge Shakespeare, *edited by F.H. Mares.*

SYNOPSIS

Leonato, Duke of Messina, father of Hero and uncle of the orphan Beatrice, is being visited by Don Pedro, Prince of Arragon, with Claudio and Benedick in his suite. With Claudio's help Don Pedro has just quelled a rebellion by his bastard brother, Don John, who now accompanies him in surly mood.

Claudio falls in love with Hero, Leonato's daughter, and with Don Pedro's help at a masked ball a marriage is soon arranged, the ceremony to take place in seven days' time.

Don John, however, no friend of Claudio, arranges for him and Don Pedro to see Hero (in reality a gentlewoman, Margaret, in disguise) engaged in a romantic assignation with Borachio, which distresses both Hero's father and her suitor.

Don Pedro, with the connivance of others, also plots to bring the teasing relationship between Beatrice and Benedick, a sworn bachelor, on to a more romantic footing. Each is tricked into believing the other in love – a state of affairs that brings about a development of genuine sympathy between them.

Borachio's boast that he was bribed a handsome sum by Don John is overheard by the night watch, and he is arrested, but through

CHECK THE BOOK

For a discussion of Shakespeare's sources, see introduction to Cambridge edition; for changes from sources to make Claudio a less engaging character, see Michael Gearin-Tosh, 'The World of *Much Ado*', in Cookson and Loughrey, eds, 1989, pp. 101–2. See **Further reading**.

Dogberry's inept handling the message is not passed on. And, on the day of the wedding, Claudio denounces Hero for unfaithfulness. She faints, and Leonato is persuaded that, for Hero's sake, it would be better to report her dead. Beatrice asks Benedick to prove his love for her by fighting Claudio in a duel, to which he agrees.

By now Leonato has begun to suspect that the accusation against his daughter Hero was false, and later this is proved to be so. As a consolation, Leonato offers Claudio his brother Antonio's daughter sight unseen as a bride the following morning. But first Claudio and Don Pedro pay homage at Hero's tomb.

The marriage takes place with the ladies masked. The bride, however, is not, after all, Antonio's daughter, but to Claudio's joy, Hero.

Benedick proposes to Beatrice, and teasingly she accepts him. The play ends with dancing.

DETAILED SUMMARIES

ACT I

SCENE 1

- The characters are introduced.
- Claudio falls in love with Hero.
- Beatrice and Benedick vow never to marry.

A messenger announces to Leonato, Governor of Messina, with his daughter, Hero, and niece, Beatrice, the imminent arrival of his friend, Don Pedro, Prince of Arragon, with his bastard brother, Don John, whose rebellion he has recently crushed, and his companions at arms, Signor Benedick, a Lord of Padua, and Count Claudio, a young Lord of Florence. Beatrice interrupts the messenger to ask after Benedick and ridicule him as soldier and lover. When Don Pedro arrives Benedick interrupts his exchange of

CHECK THE NET

For a general history of performances and discussion of text and sources see, **http://www. shakespeare. about.com/library/ weekly/aa060100a. htm.**

CHECK THE BOOK

Peter Hollindale, in 'Serious voices in a comic world', argues that Messina is the most important character, a 'society deeply vulnerable to deception and misreport', see Cookson and Loughrey, eds, 1989, p. 11.

pleasantries with Leonato with ribald jests. Beatrice attracts his attention with a gibe and the two of them, established separately as witty scorners of the opposite sex, entertain each other and the company with mocking repartee. Once Claudio is left alone with Benedick, he confesses his love for Hero. Benedick gives away the secret to Don Pedro who offers to make the match by proposing to her on behalf of Claudio while in disguise at a ball that evening.

COMMENTARY

The language is immediately elaborate and artificial. The messenger, who imitates courtly manners and style of address, uses sophisticated parallel structures, balance, **antithesis**, puns, **alliteration**, **metaphor** and **paradox**, praising Claudio, who 'hath borne himself beyond the promise of his age, doing in the figure of a lamb the feats of a lion' (lines 11–12). Leonato responds with elaborate sentimentality when told that Claudio's uncle wept with joy at the news of his success: 'how much better is it to weep at joy then to joy at weeping!' (lines 21–2). Already there are indications of Claudio's capacity for violence, so ruthlessly expressed at the altar (IV.1). References to the deceitfulness of appearances foreshadow Don John's villainy. He seeks any opportunity to 'build mischief on' (I.3.34) and will gloat as Hero weeps.

CHECK THE FILM

In his film Branagh emphasised war and love by making 'Sigh No More' the theme song and adding a scene with the women of Messina getting ready for the soldiers' arrival.

Beatrice butts in with a politely phrased question about Benedick, whom she nicknames Signor Mountanto, meaning upthrust or stuck up, instantly deflating the pompous atmosphere to demand that attention be paid to her. She launches a prolonged attack – though barbed, it is comically overstated – upon Benedick as soldier, lover and friend. She aims to get her digs in before Benedick, since the audience learns that the two are longstanding adversaries in a 'merry war' (line 45) of wit.

The messenger, who expects Hero's modest female reticence, not Beatrice's voluble assertiveness, is almost dumbstruck. Messina emerges as a strictly conventional, patriarchal society in which women are subservient. Persistent questioning and urgent repetition define Beatrice's intellectually curious, passionate and disdainful personality: 'I pray you, how many hath he killed and eaten in these wars? But how many hath he killed? – for indeed I promised to eat all of his killing' (lines 31–3). Her denigration of male pretensions to valour anticipates her bloodthirsty attack upon Claudio (IV.1).

Her wit is belligerent; she twists and turns words against their speakers. Benedick has done good service, the messenger protests; she puns on service as the food he has eaten. 'And a good soldier too, lady,' the messenger, not quite beaten, maintains, to which Beatrice retorts, converting the adverb into a preposition, 'And a good soldier to a lady, but what is he to a lord?' (line 40). When the messenger innocently protests that Benedick is 'stuffed with all honourable virtues', Beatrice instantly retorts: 'he is no less than a stuffed man' (line 43), a bawdy slight on Benedick's virility and moral hollowness. Although she remains composed and sharp, her relentless scorn conveys a real animus against men and a need to show off superior wit. Once the messenger is silenced, male aggression, the discrepancy between pretension and performance and conflict with women remain as important issues.

Leonato greets Don Pedro with elaborate politeness, and in so convoluted a manner (lines 73–5) as to sound meaningless, leaving us to question its sincerity. Benedick interrupts by teasing Leonato about his paternity and his looks. He identifies himself as a womaniser, a blunt man of few words impatient with courtly euphuism.

Benedick's affinity of temperament with Beatrice is established before she launches the first salvo in their merry war: 'I wonder that you will still be talking, Signor Benedick, nobody marks you.' The suavity of Benedick's scornful retort, 'What, my dear Lady Disdain! are you yet living' (lines 84–6), which teases her about her age, insignificance and notorious scornfulness, indicates that they are equally matched. But their conflict is more than a public show. It degenerates from clever and snide insinuation to blatant, bad-tempered vituperation. Benedick's, 'you are a rare parrot-teacher' (line 103) and Beatrice's, 'A bird of my tongue is better than a beast of yours' (line 104) are crude, childish signs that both have lost their tempers.

Claudio, the conventional idealistic lover, contrasts and clashes comically with Benedick, the scorner of women. 'Can the world buy such a jewel?' (line 134) Claudio inquires metaphorically, to which Benedick replies with deflating, mildly obscene realism, 'Yea, and a case to put it into too'. Don Pedro is Claudio's patron, older, socially superior, grateful beneficiary of his military exploits. His offer to help win Hero's hand in disguise at the masked ball typifies a strictly patriarchal society. Women are suppressed and jealously protected. Men equivocate and the truth is found by indirections.

Like Beatrice, Benedick is a show-off. He cuts Claudio short, portraying wives as faithless and husbands as cuckolds. His bestial, often lewd imagery contrasts with Claudio's romantic idealism: 'pick out my eyes with a ballad-maker's pen, and hang me up at the door of a brothel house for the sign of blind Cupid'; 'hang me in a bottle like a cat'; 'pluck off the bull's horns' (lines 186, 191 and 196). His wit has Beatrice's spontaneity and relentlessness, suggestive of passion, imagination and underlying disappointment.

All the major characters have been immediately introduced and their principal tensions and balances established. The society, though uniformly courtly, varies in nationality, character and age – Hero and Claudio youthful, Beatrice and Benedick more experienced and Don Pedro and Leonato of mature years, the men from different Italian regions. Reticent advocates of love balance garrulous scorners, romantic idealism and sententious rhetoric vie with bawdy or commonplace realism.

The opening is energetic and engaging. Claudio has fallen in love with Hero and Don Pedro will seek her hand; Beatrice and Benedick have locked horns. The language is richly varied from the courtly and artificial to the blunt and coarse. The wit in the prolific repartee, with its constant play upon words, hints at the deception of appearances and the power of illusion.

CHECK THE BOOK
For a discussion of gender, see Carol Neely, in Harold Bloom, ed., 1988, pp. 105–22. See **Further reading**.

GLOSSARY		
12	figure of a lamb the feats of a lion	the cross alliteration of f and l is a feature of the euphuistic, courtly style
17	badge of bitterness tears;	outward appearances deceive, ironically, in IV.1, not as Claudio thinks

20	kind … kindness natural or sincere; the pun masks feeling
21–2	better is it … weeping the **antithesis** hints at the possibility of deliberate and malicious deception
29–30	Cupid at the flight Roman love-god – blind winged boy with a bow and a quiver of arrows fired at random and hitting the target by chance; the flight-arrow, used for long distances
34	Faith in faith or truly
34	tax blame or criticise
34–5	be meet get even
38	excellent stomach implies Benedick would rather eat than fight
41	stuffed crammed or well stored
49	five wits common sense, imagination, fantasy, estimation and memory
49	halting limping
50–1	bear it for a difference carry a heraldic distinguishing mark
52–3	for … reasonable creature ability to keep warm being his only mark of human reason to distinguish him from his horse
58	and if (commonly so used in the text)
63	taker one who catches it
65	ere a be before he is
66	will hold friends with you will take care not to cross you
68	You will never run mad never 'catch' the Benedick, or fall in love
76	charge expense and trouble
80	for then were you a child implies Benedick is a renowned womaniser
84	his head Leonato's beard and grey or white hair
88	Lady Disdain **personification** of Beatrice as contempt implies a longstanding resentment
89	meet proper, with a **quibble** on meat
90–1	Courtesy … presence even courtesy itself would be rude to you
95	dear happiness precious good fortune

continued

CONTEXT

Witty and bawdy comedy, often performed by jesters or fools, both playing on the meanings of words, are a feature of tragedies like *Hamlet* and *King Lear* as well as comedies.

96	**pernicious suitor** an annoying lover
97	**humour** temperament
100	**scape ... face** escape having his face scratched
103	**rare parrot-teacher** outstanding chatterer, repeater of empty phrases; echoes 'stuffed man'
107	**jade's trick** like a fractious horse slipping out of the collar, he slips away from her wit
113	**be forsworn** swear in vain
122–4	**Do you ... sex?** Benedick hints that his misogyny is a pose
126	**low** short
135	**sad** serious
136–7	**Cupid ... carpenter** Benedick asks whether Claudio mocks Hero by praising qualities she lacks: Cupid was blind – good sight is needed to find a hare; Vulcan, god of fire, was not a carpenter but a blacksmith; classical allusions were signs of breeding
138	**go in the song** match your mood
147	**wear ... suspicion** wear his cap to hide the cuckold's horns of a husband with a faithless wife
148	**and thou wilt needs** if you must
149	**yoke** a wooden frame to harness pairs of oxen, implying that marriage is boring and servile
149	**sigh away Sundays** find Sundays tedious at home with wife
156	**allegiance** duty to your lord; Benedick pretends that allegiance to Don Pedro forces him to tell
157	**your grace's part** the question Don Pedro is supposed to ask
159	**If ... uttered** sulky or evasive complaint that Benedick would have blabbed if he had told him
160	**old tale** an old story containing the refrain that follows: Claudio is in love
162	**If ... change not shortly** ominous words, prompted by embarrassment, not self doubt
165	**fetch me in** trick me into a confession
174	**in the despite of beauty** in your contempt for beauty
175–6	**And ... will** keep up the pretence of despising women by sheer will power

QUESTION

'A witty play, but not a very profound one.' Consider this view of *Much Ado About Nothing*.

179–80	**recheat ... baldrick** have assembling call for hounds sounded in his forehead or hang his hunting horn in an invisible belt; unlike husbands, he will not be a cuckold
182	**fine** conclusion
182	**finer** better dressed as a bachelor
185–6	**lose ... drinking** sighing used blood which drinking replenished
186	**ballad-maker's pen** pen dedicated to writing love poetry
190	**argument** topic of discussion
191	**hang ... me** cat hung in a leather bottle or basket sometimes used for archery practice
192	**Adam** after Adam Bell, a famous archer
200	**horn-mad** raving mad
201	**Venice** famous for prostitution, sexual licence
203	**earthquake** it will take a cataclysm to change him
204	**temporise with the hours** weaken in resolution with time
209	**and so I commit you** tag from a conventional letter-ending
214	**flout old ends** mock me with old letter-endings
216	**My liege ... good** respectful address and blank verse signal change from jesting to sincere tone
220	**Hath Leonato any son?** much discussed: Claudio, coldly mercenary or merely circumspect?
222	**affect** look affectionately upon or love
228	**Have ... rooms** his mind compared to a house: all the rooms formerly occupied by war are empty and can be filled with love
233	**book of words** fashionable lovers wrote rhymes to their ladies
242	**What ... flood** a bridge need only be as wide as the river
244	**Look what** whatever
244	**'tis once** in a word
245	**fit thee** provide you with
249	**in her bosom I'll unclasp** will disclose his feelings to her privately
251	**encounter** military **metaphor** – Don Pedro compelling Hero to listen

**CHECK
THE BOOK**

For a discussion of Shakespeare's treatment of national stereotypes see Roger Sales, 1987, pp. 39–55. See **Further reading**.

SCENE 2

- Antonio thinks Don Pedro is in love with Hero.
- Leonato prepares Hero for a proposal from Don Pedro.

CONTEXT
Disguise and
misunderstanding
are features
Shakespeare
adapted from
Italian comedy.

Inside Leonato's house, his brother, Antonio, misinforms him of
Don Pedro's plan: Leonato leaves to prepare Hero for a proposal
from Don Pedro.

COMMENTARY

This scene introduces Antonio as a foolish, credulous, well-meaning
old man.

Its brevity, the surprising misinformation and bustling at its end
contrast with the spacious, leisurely opening to create a sense of
urgency and expectancy.

This is the first of many eavesdroppings, misreportings and
misconceptions. Claudio 'noted' (line 120) in Hero a beauty
Benedick could not see; Don Pedro will impersonate Claudio to
woo Hero; Antonio believes and transmits a false report:
appearances are already powerful and deceptive.

GLOSSARY	
5	they news, often plural, like tidings
6	cover like a book cover; outward appearance
9	discovered revealed
11–12	take the present ... top seize the opportunity
16	appear itself actually happens
18	peradventure perhaps
19	cry you mercy beg your pardon

SCENE 3

- The misunderstanding continues.
- Don John vows revenge on Claudio.

Don John complains of his grievances, mainly curtailed freedom, to
Conrade, a follower. Borachio, another follower, joins them. He has
eavesdropped and reports the news of Claudio's love of Hero. He
gets it slightly wrong: he claims that Don Pedro will woo her for
himself and give her to Claudio, whereas Don Pedro has planned to
disguise himself as Claudio to woo. Don John dedicates himself to
revenge against Claudio for supplanting him in his brother's favour.

Don John's resentment of Claudio – 'that young start-up hath all
the glory of my overthrow' (line 48) – and scorn of marriage –
'What is he for a fool that betroths himself to unquietness?' (line 34)
– are bitter; Benedick's gibes are not. The others have come in
triumph, Don John in defeat, discontented with a restrictive truce.
His scheming, humourless, jealous nature conforms to the
Elizabethan prejudice about bastards.

He is self-dramatising and egotistical: 'I am a plain-dealing villain'
(line 23), he boasts. His courtly language is elaborately rhetorical: 'I
must be sad when I have cause … eat when I have stomach … sleep
when I am drowsy …' (lines 10–13). They are **metaphoric** like
Beatrice's and Benedick's but with unpleasant, violent imagery,
which shocks where theirs surprises: 'I had rather be a canker in a
hedge, than a rose in his grace … I am trusted with a muzzle and
enfranchised with a clog' (lines 20–24). He is not motiveless – his
rebellion failed, Claudio succeeded, and Don Pedro suppresses him.

The setting is a private apartment where Don John plots. He boasts
of his bluntness and villainy to Conrade, who recommends
hypocritical, Machiavellian underhandedness and duplicity. He
agrees to such a strategy. Annoyed by Claudio's engagement, he
melodramatically regrets that the cook would not poison Claudio's
food.

QUESTION

Is Claudio's desire
for Hero primarily
motivated by
money?

CONTEXT

Don John is
Machiavellian:
Niccolò
Machiavelli (1469
–1527) proclaimed
the right of rulers
to advance the
interests of their
states through
amoral, cynical
manipulation of
subjects.

QUESTION

Does the melodrama associated with Don John undermine the realism of the play?

GLOSSARY

1	**What the good year** what the devil
1	**out of measure** excessively
3	**breeds** brings it about
7	**sufferance** endurance
9–10	**moral … mischief** inadequate advice for a fatal disease
16–18	**grace … yourself** botanical **metaphor** – the sunshine of his brother's grace
18	**frame** bring about
21	**blood** disposition, here of a bastard
24	**trusted … clog** compares himself to a muzzled and hobbled beast, neither trusted nor free
28	**use it only** merely cultivates his discontent
39	**for any model** as a design or scheme
39	**proper squire** handsome, refined young courtier; **ironic**
40	**Marry** truly
42	**entertained … perfumer** instructed to sweeten the atmosphere
42–3	**smoking a musty room** fumigating a stale smelling room
43	**comes me** came towards him
44	**whipped me … arras** hurried behind a wall-hanging
48	**start-up** upstart
49	**sure** loyal
53	**go prove** try or find out

Act II

Scene 1

- Don Pedro successfully woos Hero for Claudio, but his motives continue to be misunderstood.
- Don Pedro devises a plot to make Beatrice and Benedick fall in love.

In the great hall Beatrice jests about how distasteful marriage is. Leonato warns Hero to be ready to accept an offer of marriage. They mask as the guests to the ball enter. Don Pedro walks with Hero. Antonio's partner sees through his disguise and teases him, as Beatrice does Benedick. Don John pretends to mistake Claudio for Benedick and advises him to tell Don Pedro that Hero, whose love he appears to have won, is not good enough for him. Claudio blames the seductive charm of beauty for his patron's supposed treachery. Benedick, similarly deceived, teases Claudio who slinks away. Don Pedro enters and announces that he has won Hero for Claudio. Benedick, still smarting from Beatrice's criticism, leaves when she enters. Don Pedro breaks the happy news to Claudio. Leonato sets the wedding date in seven days. When Beatrice leaves, Don Pedro devises a plot to make her and Benedick fall in love.

... g for
... ball to suggest that the play was a trifling escape from reality.

COMMENTARY

Like the opening scene, the ball is extensive, varied and complex in structure and mood. It creates an air of refined grace, sophisticated merriment and romantic spaciousness. Its structure and movement are dance-like: couples and groups form, dissolve and reform as social convention dictates. Claudio and Hero and Beatrice and Benedick alternate as centres of attention. Claudio's unease about the outcome of Don Pedro's wooing by proxy is not relieved until the end of the scene.

Beatrice harps on her unsuitability and distaste for marriage and the inferiority of men: 'would it not grieve a woman to be overmastered with a piece of valiant dust' (line 44). She ridicules Benedick to his mask: 'he is the prince's jester, a very dull fool, only his gift is in devising impossible slanders' (line 103), indicating that she knows his identity. Nettled, Benedick taunts Claudio for succumbing to Hero only to lose her to his patron. Don Pedro displays a passion for trickery. Having wooed Hero unnecessarily, he exerts himself to match Benedick and Beatrice.

The masked wooing, Claudio's apprehensiveness and Don Pedro's proposed matchmaking highlight the illusion in Claudio's love and prepare us for his disillusionment. The audience is watching

CHECK THE BOOK

Nicholas Potter in 'Romance and realism', argues that the play makes a clear distinction between the world of courtly love and the world of realism and that masking focuses attention on identity as surface appearance, see Cookson and Loughrey, eds, 1989, p. 56.

QUESTION

At what point would you have Beatrice recognise Benedick in order to torment him?

Claudio watching Don Pedro, which adds to our sense of romance and drama as artifice and illusion.

The light, gay dialogue is darkened not only by Don John's intervention but also by the increasing acrimony of Beatrice's and Benedick's 'merry war' (I.1.45) and a growing conviction of the difficulty of sexual relations.

GLOSSARY

4	heart-burned heart burn caused by Don John's sour expression; Beatrice, like Benedick (IV.1), distrusts Don John
6	image statue; suggestive of cold conventionality
15	shrewd shrewish; sharp
16	curst perverse; ill-tempered
17	lessen God's sending reduce what God has given me
18–20	God ... horn an unruly woman too curst will not cuckold a husband, since no man will marry her and give her his horn (member)
21	Just just so
21–2	at him praying to God
23–4	lie in the woollen without sheets, in scratchy blankets
30–1	earnest of the bearward as an advance payment to the bear-keeper
31	lead his apes into hell proverbial fate if women died old maids
42	fitted matched; slightly pejorative and bawdy
47	match in my kindred marry a close relative
54	first suit wooing
56	ancientry elderly dignity
61	walk a bout dance
67	favour face
67	defend forbid
69	Philemon's roof ... Jove Jove and Mercury, disguised as mortals, visited house of Philemon and Baucis, a peasant couple, who welcomed them
70	thatched bearded
86	so ill-well oxymoron: seeming 'ill' requires art

90	**Go to, mum** Come, say no more
96–7	***The Hundred Merry Tales*** a collection of crudely comic tales, implying that she lacks originality
106	**angers them** when he makes offensive jokes about them
107	**boarded** nautical term – come along close with intent of boarding in an attack; bawdy overtones, hinting at sexual attraction for Benedick
111	**partridge wing** little meat on it; suggests Benedick hasn't much of an appetite
117	**visor** masked person
127	**banquet** a dessert course – fruit, wines, sweet meats
137	**accident of hourly proof** occurrence proved true every hour
143–4	**willow … garland** emblem of unrequited love
143	**county** count
154	**poor hurt fowl … sedges** sympathetic image of a wounded bird fleeing to the undergrowth
159	**so gives me out** causes such things to be said about me
161	**Lady Fame** personification of rumour
162	**lodge in a warren** a gamekeeper's lodge in a park would be lonely and therefore melancholy
172	**amiss** in vain
177–8	**If … honestly** if what you say proves true, then you speak honourably
184–5	**duller than a great thaw** roads impassable forcing people to stay home
185	**impossible conveyance** incredible skill or trickery
186	**man at the mark** man who stood near the target to tell archers how close they were
188	**terminations** terms to describe me
190	**all that Adam … transgressed** Adam had dominion over all creation before eating of the tree of knowledge
193–4	**scholar … conjure her** a scholar would exorcise her and send her back to hell
201	**tooth-picker** toothpick, sign of affectation
202	**Prester John** legendary Christian king of Asian country
203	**Great Cham** emperor of China

continued

QUESTION

'The play confirms Benedick's fear that fidelity and harmony in sexual relations are impossible to maintain.' How helpful do you find this view to your understanding of *Much Ado About Nothing*?

Scene 1 continued

204	**Harpy** fierce bird-like monster with beautiful female face; expresses Benedick's anger
212	**double heart ... single** possible hint of earlier betrayal by Benedick
223–4	**civil ... complexion** sober in behaviour and with a yellow complexion, token of jealousy
238–9	**windy side of care** away from care
241	**goes everyone ... world** everyone is getting married
242	**sunburnt** unattractive
245	**getting** begetting
254–5	**star danced** astrological explanation of cheerful temper
264	**out of suit** from courting her
273	**breathing** breathing space or interval
280	**watchings** sleepless nights

SCENE 2

- Borachio and Don John devise a cruel plot to deceive Claudio.
- Borochio's friend Margaret will impersonate Hero.

CONTEXT

Slander is a serious crime in many Shakespearean plays.

In another room, away from the ball, Borachio devises for Don John a scheme to prevent Hero's and Claudio's marriage. On the eve of the wedding he will persuade Margaret, a gentlewoman in love with him, to express her feelings from a chamber window as if she were Hero. Don John, having accused Hero, will bring Claudio and Don Pedro to witness the scene and confirm her infidelity.

COMMENTARY

Don John's expressions of aggression and impatience – 'I am sick in displeasure at him' (line 4) – and a 1,000 ducat reward betray festering hatred and desperation to stop Claudio's marriage. Don John is ready to be led by Borachio, who is ambitious, unscrupulous and confident of his absolute control over Margaret.

In its unrelieved villainy and cynical imagery – 'poison of that lies in you to temper' (line 17), 'be cozened with the semblance of a maid' (line 29), 'be cunning in the working' (line 39), the scene is crudely melodramatic.

This cabal of Don John, Borachio and Conrade balances, opposes and contrasts the comradeship of Don Pedro, Claudio and Benedick. As Don Pedro has 'bestowed much honour' (I.1.7) on Claudio, so Don John rewards Borachio with money. Don Pedro secured Hero's hand for his protégé, whereas Borachio, the protégé, plots to disgrace Hero for his patron, the baser for his reliance upon an underling.

In a society dominated by codes, appearances and conventions, the villainy depends appropriately upon the appearance of corruption. The excessive emphasis upon sexual purity creates an exploitable insecurity in the romantic lover. He springs his trap on the susceptible Don Pedro and Claudio, when Benedick, the realist, is absent.

CHECK THE BOOK
Mick Mangan examines the variety and function of 'jokes, tricks and witticisms', distinguishing the 'benevolent' from the 'malevolent' and discovering in the jokes about cuckolds 'an anxiety about woman's sexual licence', in 'A College of Wit Crackers', Cookson and Loughrey, eds, 1989, p. 88 and p. 96.

GLOSSARY	
4	medicinable healing (his resentment)
14	unseasonable instant untimely or inappropriate moment
17	temper concoct
20	contaminated stale soiled merchandise; corrupt prostitute
27	intend a kind of zeal pretend to have an earnest concern
27	as in love of as if you were concerned for
28	cozened with … maid cheated with deceiving appearance of a virgin
31	trial evidence
31	instances proof
32–3	hear Margaret … Claudio Claudio will think his love is mocked
36–7	jealousy … assurance mere suspicion will become certainty

CHECK THE FILM
Through the Sicilian mafia setting in his 1965 film of *Much Ado*, Franco Zeffirelli was able to imply the importance of virginity and vengeance in a way that explained Claudio's behaviour.

SCENE 3

- Benedick is tricked into believing that Beatrice is in love with him.
- So falls in love with her.

In the orchard Benedick bemoans Claudio's transformation from soldier to lover. Could love so change him, he wonders, complacently reviewing his immunity to various female charms and conjuring up a vision of the ideal woman incorporating all possible virtues of mind and body. He hides when Don Pedro, Claudio and Leonato approach. Balthasar sings a song about the suffering men's inconstancy causes women. Having spied Benedick eavesdropping in his hiding place, his three friends express their pity for Beatrice, dying for love which she hides for fear of his scorn. They flatteringly review Benedick's virtues but deplore his pride and contempt for women. Once they have gone, Benedick in a **soliloquy** admits that his faults should be amended, Beatrice be pitied and loved, that he is in love, must settle down, marry and father children. When she calls him to dinner, he greets her with incomprehensible civility and interprets her least encouraging remarks as evidence of love.

CONTEXT

The soliloquy is used in this play and others to reveal a character's innermost thoughts.

COMMENTARY

After Don John's malicious plotting to deceive, Don Pedro, Claudio and Leonato deceive Benedick benevolently into loving Beatrice. The gaiety with which the prank is performed and the complete sincerity with which Benedick is taken in contrasts with the stiff unpleasantness of the previous scene. Amidst the gaiety, however, are hints of sadness: illusion may bring Beatrice and Benedick together, but it is about to divide Claudio and Hero. One plot is propelled towards tragedy, which the comic trajectory of the other softens.

Benedick's first soliloquy (lines 7–28) in which he marvels at Claudio's transformation from soldier and scoffer to lover – 'I do much wonder, that one man seeing how much another is a fool …

will after he hath laughed at such shallow follies in others, become the argument of his own scorn, by falling in love' – is comical and ironic, as he is about to be tricked himself. He complacently ponders his immunity to binding female charms, 'one woman is fair, yet I am well; another is wise, yet I am well', and reviews the impossible collection of female virtues required to entrap him – 'till all graces be in one woman, one woman shall not be in my grace'. This is pride and we look forward to his fall no less than we dread Claudio's. It is amusingly ironic that mere hearsay entraps him. When in his second soliloquy (lines 181–200) he rationalises his sudden love for Beatrice – 'I did never think to marry, I must not seem proud', 'the world must be peopled' – expresses his pity – 'love me? It must be requited', 'I will be horribly in love with her' – and admiration for her – 'the lady is fair … and virtuous … and wise' – and cringes as he imagines the mockery such a famous scorner of women will receive – 'I may have some odd quirks and remnants of wit broken on me' – the comedy reaches its peak.

Balthasar's melancholy song has created a conducive mood: 'Sigh no more, ladies, sigh no more, / Men were deceivers ever' (lines 53–4). Benedick is about to be inconstant in abandoning his misogyny, Claudio in dishonouring his adored Hero and Leonato in disowning her.

Sexual desire and illusion prompt Benedick's love, confirming that Cupid is blind, love irrational. Benedick's distortion of his own former misogyny and of Beatrice's summons to dinner is comical. As a lover, Benedick, once cynical and ironic, though generously witty, becomes ingenuous and sincere. His misogyny was an illusion arresting his emotional development until Don Pedro's deception released it.

 QUESTION

What hints are there in the first soliloquy that Benedick is discontented being a bachelor and in the second what are the key features attracting him to Beatrice?

CONTEXT

In Branagh's film the song, 'Sigh No More, Ladies', brought out the gaiety of Messina society and the sadness of the woman's lot.

GLOSSARY	
5	am here already it is as good as done
9	argument object
16	turned orthography speaks in an elaborate, flowery style
19	transform me … oyster shut me up in moody silence like a clam
	continued

Scene 3 continued

CHECK THE BOOK
Charles Moseley, 'Men Were Deceivers Ever', connects the song with the 'notion that deception, deliberately encouraging misprision, is part of (at least male) human nature', Cookson and Loughrey, eds, 1989, p. 44.

20	**made an oyster of me** utterly undid me
23	**come in my grace** win my acceptance
25	**cheapen** bargain for
26	**noble ... angel** (pun) names of Elizabethan coins
34	**fit ... pennyworth** give Benedick more than he bargains for
38	**witness ... excellency** always the sign of excellence
39	**put a strange face on** pretend not to know
46	**Do it in notes** (pun) musical notes; be brief
48	**crochets** quarter notes, whims or trifles
49	**Note notes ... nothing** Don Pedro complains that Balthasar is supplying empty verbal conceits for music
51	**sheep's guts** lute strings were made of sheep guts
51	**hale** draw
51	**horn** hunting horn
60	**hey nonny nonny** meaningless phrase hinting at erotic joys of nothing, or female genitalia
61	**no mo** no more in number
62	**dumps** mournful moods and solemn tunes
63	**fraud** faithlessness
64	**leavy** leafy
71	**for a shift** as a makeshift, trick
74	**as lief** rather
74	**night-raven** raven's croak foreshadowed disaster
83	**stalk on, the fowl sits** start your hunting, the game bird (Benedick) has settled
88	**Sits the wind ... corner** is that really the way things are
90–1	**past ... thought** it is unbelievable but true
108	**ta'en th'infection** he has fallen for the trick
120	**between the sheet** paper and bed linen implying Beatrice wants to sleep with Benedick
121	**That** yes, that's it
129	**ecstasy** frenzy, passion
132–3	**It were good ... it** It would be good if Benedick learned of it from somebody else as she will not reveal it
136	**And he should ... alms** if he did, it would be a good deed
140	**blood** passion

144	dotage infatuation
145	daffed all other respects put aside all other considerations
150	bate abate, yield
152	make tender offer
154	contemptible contemptuous, scornful
160	Hector Trojan warrior hero
161–2	avoids … fear risks giving the game away
166	large jests coarse wisecracks
178	and no such matter without any basis for their opinion
181	conference … borne the conversation was conducted seriously
183	have their full bent are stretched to the limit like a bow before the arrow is fired
189	reprove disprove or deny
192	quirks quips, quibbles, gibes
195	sentences epigrams, pithy proverbs, witty sayings
196	career of his humour course of his inclination
206–7	upon a knife's … withal as swallowing a knife point and being choked like a jackdaw
212	Jew faithless rascal

ACT III

SCENE 1

- Beatrice is similarly tricked.
- She vows to love Benedick.

The day before the wedding, Beatrice is tricked. Hero tells Margaret to fetch Beatrice to the orchard with the news that she is being talked about. As Beatrice eavesdrops, Hero and Ursula lament Benedick's suffering for love of her. Calling her proud and scornful, they say Benedick should resist his inclination and consider it futile to tell

CHECK THE FILM

In the BBC video setting of *Much Ado*, the gulling scenes outdoors between and behind hedges made falling in love seem natural and inevitable.

Beatrice she is loved. Afterwards they discuss Hero's wedding. In a soliloquy, Beatrice is transformed: she accepts that she is too proud and vows to take pity on Benedick by loving him.

COMMENTARY

Beatrice eavesdrops in the same orchard as Benedick, who, she overhears, is wasting away for a love he will keep secret for fear of being mocked. Her sharp, scornful tongue is deplored, her self-love criticised and her wit and beauty complimented.

This scene lacks the impact of the previous one. It is half as long and Beatrice's fall from disdain seems less great or funny. The incomplete parallel limits the artificiality and preserves an element of realism while preparing gradually for the darkening of Don John's successful plot. The illusory quality of romantic love is enhanced: a piece of drama, an illusion within the illusion, is performed which kindles love.

Blank verse elevates Beatrice's love. She does not voice Benedick's anxiety about reputation; her conversion is more complete and her immediate reaction is to requite him. The scene therefore has less movement, is more subdued and more dignified, hinting at superior female delicacy and refinement.

In Beatrice's deception, free of her cousin's domination or her father's supervision, Hero's character emerges. She delivers a flowery, complex speech about the beauties of the orchard, which implies some knowledge of court intrigue: 'the pleachèd bower, / Where honeysuckles ripened by the sun, / Forbid the sun to enter: like favourites, / Made proud by princes, that advance their pride, / Against that power that bred it' (lines 7–11). She knows about love, often the product of rumour – 'little Cupid's crafty arrow ... only wounds by hearsay' (lines 22–3). She is totally in command, showing a keen understanding of Beatrice's character and the ploys that will reduce her to love-sickness for Benedick. Almost mute in public, she speaks with warmth, at length and with poetic dignity. This development of her character enhances the **pathos** of her later dishonour.

CONTEXT

Beatrice expresses her love in strictly formal Elizabethan, **iambic pentameter** verse in an *ababcdcdee* rhyme scheme.

QUESTION

What are the similarities and differences in the way Beatrice and Benedick express their new love in their soliloquies?

GLOSSARY

3	**Proposing** conversing
4	**Ursley** Ursula
10	**advance their pride** assert themselves insolently; like Don John against his brother or Claudio against Hero
12	**office** task or role
24	**like a lapwing** a bird of proverbial craftiness that lures hunters away from its nest by running, as though injured
27	**golden oars** fins
30	**couchèd** hidden, lowered into a crouching position
35	**coy** contemptuous, looking down on others
36	**As haggards ... rock** as wild and disdainful as female hawks
38	**new trothèd lord** newly engaged husband-to-be
42	**wrestle with affection** try to overcome his feelings
52	**Misprising** undervaluing
54	**All matter ... weak** all discourse except her display of wit seems weak
55	**take ... affection** take on any appearance or notion of love
61	**spell him backward** misrepresent him
63	**an antic** a grotesque figure
64	**a lance ill-headed** a dully tipped spear
65	**an agate** tiny figures cut into agate stones; hence, a dwarf
67	**block moved with none** unresponsive to any winds
70	**simpleness** integrity, plain honesty
72	**from all fashions** out of step with everyone
84	**honest** innocent
86	**ill word ... liking** ironically prophetic – Don John's slander poisons Claudio's love
90	**prized to have** valued for having
101	**every day, tomorrow** every day, from tomorrow
104	**limed** caught with bird lime
105	**haps** chance
110	**lives behind ... such** is gained by following such a path of contempt and maiden pride
114	**band** bond

CHECK THE FILM

In Branagh's film of *Much Ado*, an explicit sexual scene witnessed by an innocent Claudio makes his vindictiveness more understandable.

SCENE 2

- Don Pedro and Claudio make fun of the lovesick Benedick.
- Don John claims he knows Hero has been unfaithful.

Inside the house, Don Pedro and Claudio make fun of Benedick for being morosely in love and changed in dress and demeanour. Benedick protests that he has tooth-ache. He asks to speak to Leonato in private, presumably about Beatrice, and they leave together. Don John enters and claims to know that Hero has been unfaithful. He offers to make Don Pedro and Claudio witnesses to a meeting with her lover that night. Claudio vows to disgrace her if the report is true; Don Pedro vows to back him up.

COMMENTARY

The descent from the comedy of Benedick trying to pass off his love-sickness as tooth-ache to the threatened tragedy of Hero's slander is rapid. His discomfort is amusing: he, who teased Claudio, is trying to hide what he, Don Pedro and the audience know.

Appearances deceive. Illusions or allusions have tricked Benedick into loving Beatrice. In this scene, his sullen demeanour, recent shave, foreign fashions and perfume are irrefutable signs of love-sickness.

The generous teasing of Benedick ensures that we retain some affection for Claudio and Don Pedro and highlights the contrasting deviousness of Don John. His ambiguous language seduces just as double meanings and innuendo had tricked Benedick. Initially self-deprecation and remorse win their sympathy. The indefinite, anodyne 'disloyal' (line 76) implies reluctance to accuse Hero, which makes the brisk offer of immediate visual evidence irresistible.

Don Pedro, Claudio and Don John make melodramatic exclamations one after another, indicating, **ironically**, how they who tricked Benedick have been no less suddenly transformed.

QUESTION

Can you come up with reasons why the men are so easily tricked into believing that Hero has been unfaithful?

GLOSSARY

1	**consummate** completed
8	**cut Cupid's bowstring** prevented Cupid firing arrows, which is why he is happily unaffected by love
8	**hangman** rascal or rogue (Cupid)
12	**sadder** more serious
21	**humour or a worm** supposed causes of tooth decay, humour – a bodily fluid
22	**grief** pain
25–6	**Dutchman ... Frenchman** fashionable Englishmen were known for constantly changing clothes
27	**slops** loose, baggy breeches
28	**no doublet** all cape in the Spanish style
35	**stuffed tennis balls** beard hair was used for this purpose
37	**civet** modish perfume
37	**smell him out** see if he really is in love
42	**paint himself** use cosmetics
42–3	**For the ... of him** that is what people are saying about him
44	**Nay, but his ... spirit** No, that's just his way of joking
44–5	**crept into ... by stops** Benedick has turned lover – love songs were accompanied by the lute
50	**ill conditions** bad habits
51	**buried ... upwards** her only death is to be buried under Benedick's body
54	**hobby-horses** buffoons
60	**Good den** God give you good evening
71	**aim better at me** judge me better
73	**suit ill-spent** effort wasted
82	**warrant** proof
88	**trust ... know** if you are afraid to trust what you see, don't confess what you know
95–6	**bear it coldly** proceed calmly
97	**untowardly turned** perversely pushed in the opposite direction
98	**mischief** misfortune

CHECK THE BOOK

Brean Hammond, 'Suspicion in Sicily', argues that 'the Sicilian court is compromised by a lack of trust that has become endemic, that breeds suspicion and results in an exceptionally fragile set of alliances and misalliances', Cookson and Loughrey, 1989, p. 64.

SCENE 3

- The Watch overhear Borachio boasting to Conrade of his part in Don John's plot.
- They arrest them.

After midnight on a Messina street Dogberry, the master constable, organises the Watch. He leaves and Borachio comes by boasting to Conrade that he has earned a thousand ducats from Don John by making Claudio think Hero unfaithful. The Watch overhear the account and arrest both of them.

COMMENTARY

Dogberry and the Watch are introduced both to relieve and screw up the tension on the eve of the wedding. They broaden the picture of Messina society. Their lack of education and simplicity contrast with the sophistication and deviousness of the aristocracy. Their buffoonery lightens the atmosphere and hints at a happy ending even as the arrest of Borachio and Conrade leaves us suspended: will the truth come to light before Hero is disgraced?

> **CONTEXT**
>
> Productions have brought out the comedy of the Watch in such different ways as having them ride bicycles or be native East Indians.

Dogberry and Verges are a comic combination, one a large, rotund, overbearing know-all and the other a small, wizened, modest incompetent. When Dogberry tries impressing the Watch, his series of **malapropisms**, use of the wrong word for another similar in sound or sense, makes him ridiculous: 'Who think you is the most desartless man to be constable?' (line 8) he asks, meaning deserving, yet **ironically** underlining their ineptitude; 'To be a well-favoured man is a gift of Fortune, but to write and read comes by nature' (lines 13–14) he expounds, when the opposite is the case. His instructions are nonsense: the Watch is to interfere or apprehend none of the drunk and disorderly, 'let them alone till they are sober' (line 39) and may sleep on the job, 'I cannot see how sleeping should offend' (line 35). Their success in uncovering the plot is fortuitous and ironic, since cunning aristocracy's spying comes to nothing.

The Watch eavesdropping on Borachio and Conrade reminds us of the orchard scenes. Dogberry's stupid self-importance crudely parodies Benedick, his opposite in his linguistic incompetence, but counterpart in making a word mean whatever he wants. These ironic parallels help unify the play. The havoc Dogberry lets loose corresponds to the passions the aristocracy cannot control. Gentle satire on the Elizabethan Watch and the vanity of power is made as court wit and the high style are parodied.

Borachio introduces the theme of the decay of morals to excuse his own greed. 'What a deformed thief this fashion is' (line 101), he says, touching upon the superficiality of Messina's social values. When the first watchman misunderstands this as a comment on a 'vile thief, this seven year, a goes up and down like a gentleman' (line 103) Shakespeare is satirising the underlying corruption of a glittering society.

> **? QUESTION**
>
> How would you distinguish the witty language of Beatrice and Benedick from the comedy created by Dogberry's language?

GLOSSARY

2	salvation **(malapropism)** damnation
5	allegiance (malapropism) treason
7	give them their charge explain their duties to them
8	desartless (malapropism) deserving; but actually meaning lacking in merit
13	good name sea coal – high quality coal that came from Newcastle south by sea
13	well-favoured handsome or blessed
13	gift of fortune inversion – beauty is a gift of nature, reading and writing of fortune
19	senseless (malapropism) sensible
21	comprehend (malapropism) apprehend
31	tolerable (malapropism) intolerable
32–3	We will … watch a dig at the famous ineptitude of the Watch
32	belongs to is the proper thing for
34	ancient experienced
36	bills pikes or halberds, their weapons
45	meddle or make mingle or have to do

continued

Scene 3 continued

52	**hang a dog by my will** hang a dog willingly; animals could be charged with offences
59	**calf** infant
61	**present** (malapropism) represent
63	**stay** arrest
70–1	**and there … chances** if anything of importance happens
71–2	**keep your … own** be discreet
77	**coil** hubbub
77	**vitigant** (malapropism) vigilant
82	**Mass** by the holy mass, an oath
82	**scab** villain
86	**penthouse** shed or sloping porch
87	**like a true drunkard** Borachio's name means drunkard; also the proverb, in wine the truth
88	**stand close** be quiet
93	**be so rich** pay so much
94	**make what price** ask what price
96	**unconfirmed** inexperienced
97	**nothing to a man** tells nothing about whoever wears them
103	**a has … gentleman** satirises upper-class hypocrisy
106	**vane** weathervane
108	**turns about** plays havoc with
109	**Pharaoh's soldiers** Pharaoh, king of Egypt, pursuing the escaping Israelites
110	**reechy** filthy, smoke-grimed
110	**god Bel's priests** Bel's overthrow by Daniel in King Cyrus of Persia's reign
111	**shaven Hercules** confused with Samson, shaved by Delilah
112	**codpiece … club** codpiece – genital pouch at front of men's breeches to hold the club
116	**shifted out** deviated from; (pun) shift as shirt
120	**leans me out** leaned out of the window for him
122	**possessed** convinced, evilly influenced
135	**right** right honourable or worthy
136	**recovered** (malapropism) discovered

QUESTION

Some critics have complained that the farcical comedy of Dogberry and the Watch is an irrelevance and distraction from the serious issues of love and fidelity in the play. What are your views?

136	lechery (malapropism) treachery
142	obey (malapropism) order
144–5	goodly ... bills very useful, being arrested by these men's halberds
146	in question sought after

SCENE 4

- Preparations are made for Hero's wedding.
- Beatrice is love-sick.

A little before five the next morning, Hero is choosing her wedding attire with Margaret and Ursula, her gentlewomen. Margaret teases Hero about losing her virginity, reminding her that it is common to all women in marriage, whatever their station. Beatrice enters, sick with love, which she calls a cold, and is teased. The men arrive and Hero has to dress for the church.

COMMENTARY

The scene parallels Benedick's teasing by Claudio and Don Pedro (III.2). Margaret adopts a bawdier version of Beatrice's wit. When Hero complains that her heart is heavy with apprehension, Margaret replies, ''Twill be heavier soon by the weight of a man' (line 20), and when Hero primly remonstrates, she protests, 'is there any harm in the heavier for a husband?' (line 26). Natural feelings, she implies, are repressed in the court. She recommends, 'distilled *Carduus benedictus*' (line 54) for Beatrice's alleged cold, adding that falling in love is common, 'methinks you look with your eyes as other women do' (line 67). The ease with which Beatrice is outwitted underlines the universal, binding force of love.

Hero's anxiety about her appearance at the ceremony and conduct on her wedding night is poignant, since we know that Borachio has successfully played his trick on Don Pedro and Claudio. The Watch

> **CONTEXT**
>
> In medieval romance, a source, and Shakespearean comedy, love is often associated with disease and madness.

has arrested the villains, but whether they will be brought to justice in time is doubtful.

Throughout the play, intimate scenes are played off against public scenes to develop character and create sympathy. The conflict between public and private morality is central: Hero's denunciation dishonours her accusers.

? QUESTION

Can you reconcile the bawdy with the romantic in this play?

GLOSSARY	
5	**rebato** kind of stiff collar or ruff
10	**tire** complete headdress, including false hair and ornament
15	**cuts** made in the edge of a garment for ornament
15–16	**down ... side sleeves** the first were full-length fitted sleeves, the second loose, open sleeves
16	**round underborne** trimmed underneath
17	**quaint** elegant, dainty
24	**saving your reverence** phrase of apology
25	**and bad ... speaking** if a dirty mind does not twist innocent words
28	**light** sexually playful
33	**Clap's ...** *Love* change your tune at once to the joy of love
33	**without a burden** lightly, without a bass part, or without a man
35	**Ye light ... heels** Beatrice insinuates that Margaret will lie down with any man
36	**barns** (pun) bairns, children
39	**heigh ho** a sigh
41	**H** ache, sometimes pronounced aitch
42	**turned Turk** become a renegade, change beliefs in love
43	**star** Pole or fixed star
44	**trow** I wonder
47, 48	**stuffed** blocked nose or pregnant
49–50	**professed apprehension** laid claim to wit
52	**cap** fool's cap
54	*Carduus benedictus* holy thistle, a cure for all afflictions

55	**qualm** sudden sickness
57	**moral** hidden meaning
61	**list** please or wish
66	**eats … grudging** he now has become a normal man and readily eats the diet of love
70	**Not a false gallop** I speak the truth

SCENE 5

- Dogberry and Verges come to tell Leonato the truth before the wedding.
- Leonato fails to grasp the meaning of their talk.

Dogberry and Verges come to tell Leonato, busy with last-minute wedding preparations, about the men the Watch arrested. Their governor so awes them that they speak in such a roundabout way that Leonato has not ascertained what Borachio has done before he leaves for the ceremony. His parting words are that they should examine the men themselves.

COMMENTARY

Dogberry's and Verges's difficulty coming to the point leaves scope for interpretation: they could be drunk – Leonato offers them wine – overawed by speaking to their governor at home or trying to impress with their version of courtly circumlocution. The scene both amuses and frustrates: the constables' incoherence and Leonato's anxiety about the wedding prevent a happy resolution.

CONTEXT

It is dramatically ironic that Leonato's inability to bring Dogberry to the point has tragic consequences.

GLOSSARY		
Sd	*Headborough*	parish constable, local officer
2	confidence	he means conference
3	decerns (**malapropism**)	concerns
8	Goodman	title for man below the rank of gentleman
		continued

9	blunt (malapropism) sharp
13	odorous (malapropism) odious or hateful
13	palabras (Spanish) a few words
16	tedious as a king he thinks tedious means rich
20	exclamation (malapropism) acclamation
23	fain know like to know
24	excepting he means respecting
25	ha' ta'en have arrested
25	arrant out and out
27	world to see wonder to behold
28	God's a good man God is good
28–9	and two ... behind if two men ride on one horse, there can be only one leader
33	Gifts that God give smug, affecting humility
35	comprehended (malapropism) apprehended
36	aspitious (malapropism) suspicious
40	suffigance (malapropism) sufficient
50	noncome bewilderment, out of their wits
51	excommunication (malapropism) communication or examination

ACT IV

SCENE 1

- Hero is denounced at her wedding.
- She faints, and is declared dead.
- Beatrice asks Benedick to prove his love by killing Claudio.

The wedding ceremony begins. Leonato is anxious for it to come off swiftly and smoothly. When interrupted, he does not understand. Eventually Claudio takes over the service, denouncing Hero at the

QUESTION

It has been said that 'the best comedy comes perilously close to tragedy'. In what ways can you apply this statement to *Much Ado about Nothing*?

altar for unfaithfulness and sexual promiscuity. He is backed up by
Don Pedro and Don John, with whom he leaves after Hero has
fainted under his and her father's onslaught. Benedick, Beatrice and
the Friar hold back. The Friar has detected signs of innocence in
Hero and persuades Leonato to announce her death to gain her
sympathy, lessen her disgrace and allow her to start a new life in
hiding. Claudio's feelings might also change. Benedick remains to
console a tearful Beatrice, which leads to mutual confessions of love.
When he asks what he can do to prove his love, she demands that he
kill Claudio. Initially incredulous and reluctant, afraid of losing her,
he eventually agrees.

CHECK THE BOOK
See Roger Sales,
1987, for a
discussion of the
patriarchal values
underlying Claudio's
and Leonato's
actions.

COMMENTARY

The Claudio–Hero, Beatrice–Benedick, Don John plots come
together, all with successful deceptions. Claudio rejects Hero
brutally, from the sarcastic 'rich and precious gift' (line 23) to 'Give
not this rotten orange to your friend / She's but the sign and
semblance of her honour' (lines 27–8) her outer beauty concealing
corruption within. Gestures from placing Hero's hand back in
Leonato's to his throwing her to the floor have accompanied these
words. In the short prefatory speeches Claudio's indignation has
raged and does not subside before he leaves. He refers bitterly to
her virginal freshness, 'like a maid she blushes' (line 29) as an evil
temptation, when it is **ironically** the sign of her honour. Don Pedro,
providing cowardly support, twists Hero's attempted answer, 'Why
then you are no maiden' (line 81), and Don John hypocritically
regrets her 'much misgovernment' (line 92). Claudio plays on words
self-righteously, 'Oh Hero! What a hero hadst thou been, / If half
thy outward graces had been placed / About thy thoughts and
counsels of thy heart?' (lines 93–5) This speech is ironic: when
Claudio had called her 'the sweetest lady that ever I looked on'
(I.1.139), Benedick had replied, 'I see no such matter' (I.1.140). His
vision of her dishonour is no less illusory than his earlier love.

Leonato, at first dumb-struck by the unexpected accusation at the
climactic moment of his only daughter's marriage, unleashes an even
more savage denunciation of Hero, wishing that she had never been
born or not recover from her swoon or threatening to kill her
himself to vitiate dishonour. His language is repetitious, overstated

QUESTION

Can you justify
the cruelty of
Claudio's rejection
of Hero?

and melodramatic – a grief-stricken father, his veneer of elderly
gentleness torn away. 'I' and 'mine' reverberate, exposing him as
possessive, little concerned for Hero's feelings, preoccupied with his
own reputation. The male ideal of honour excludes femininity. He
has clung to his illusion about Hero, his tenderness for the lady
herself destroyed.

Knowledge of Hero's innocence and expectation that the Watch will
bring the truth to light soften the scene. The Friar sees rightly that
Hero is innocent. The upward movement continues when Benedick
comforts and pledges his love to Beatrice. One deception has
divided, the other two unite, and from Hero's suffering the love of
Benedick and Beatrice is cemented. The tenderness, humility and
sincerity of his, 'Lady Beatrice, have you wept all this while?' (line
248) and 'I do love nothing in the world so well as you, is it not
strange?' (lines 259–60) distances us from Claudio's denunciation.
The equally modest circumlocution with which Beatrice tries both
to conceal and reveal her feelings, 'I loved nothing so well as you,
but believe me not, and yet I lie not' (line 262), makes her
unqualified, 'I love you with so much of my heart, that none is left
to protest' (line 276) a comically joyful triumph which soothes the
pain of Hero's disgrace. Another reversal occurs immediately when
Benedick plays the conventional lover to ask, 'Come bid me do
anything for thee', and she replies simply, 'Kill Claudio'. The way
an actress delivers this line determines her interpretation of the
character. Benedick's 'Ha, not for the wide world' (lines 278–80)
exposes initially the gulf between her world of women and his of
men. Her convincing him to challenge Claudio, 'Enough, I am
engaged' (line 313) announces his defection from male privilege and
honour to absolute commitment to Beatrice's concept of justice and
friendship: 'You dare easier be friends with me, than fight with mine
enemy' (line 288). Her character is unchanged: no man will put a
woman down with impunity; she will dominate, which, though
comic, makes Benedick a better man.

QUESTION

How would you
have Beatrice say,
'Kill Claudio' and
what would you
have it indicate
about her
character?

Insistence upon vengeance is consistent with Beatrice's passionate
defiance. She has attacked male effeminacy and resents Hero's
slander as bullying the defenceless. 'Would it not grieve a woman to
be overmastered with a piece of valiant dust?' (II.1.43–4)

foreshadows, 'Oh God that I were a man! I would eat his heart in the market place' (lines 294–5). She insists that Benedick commit himself to his feelings, rather than the male code which has made Don Pedro, Claudio and Leonato selfish, unfeeling and hypocritical.

CONTEXT

It is thought that Shakespeare's audience would have found comical a woman trying to act in a dominant and even bloodthirsty way.

GLOSSARY

8	**inward** secret
28	**sign** echoes Claudio's III.2.32; semblance: either fake imitation or genuine likeness
29	**maid** innocent virgin
30	**what authority ... truth** what appearance of authority and truth
31	**withal** with
32	**modest evidence** evidence of modesty
36	**luxurious** lascivious or lustful
39	**approvèd wanton** proven whore
40	**proof** test or trial of Hero
45	**extenuate ... sin** lessen the guilt of pre-marital sex
46	**too large** improper
51	**Dian in her orb** Diana, the moon (orb), goddess of chastity
52	**blown** come into full bloom
54	**Venus** goddess of love
56	**wide** wide of the mark, mistakenly
59	**stale** prostitute
68	**kindly power** natural authority as her father
72	**catechising** formal questioning in religion particularly
76	**Hero itself** the very name of Hero
86	**liberal** frank beyond honesty or decency, gross
92	**much misgovernment** most serious misconduct
96	**most foul, most fair** beautiful on the outside but corrupt within
97	**pure impiety ... purity** oxymoron expressing difference between her appearance and what he thinks she is
99	**conjecture** doubt or suspicion
101	**never ... gracious** beauty will never again be pleasing

continued

CHECK THE BOOK

Cedric Watts, 'The World of Much Ado', argues that it is a fault of the play 'that Hero is too good for this gullible lover whose capacity for distrust makes his love seem callow and fickle', Cookson and Loughrey, eds, 1989, p. 111.

115	printed in her blood shown by her blushes, stamped on her life
119	on … reproaches immediately after reproaching you
121	Chid I … frame Did I blame nature for giving me only one child?
125	issue child
131	I myself … mine in my own eyes, I counted for nothing, compared to the value I placed on her
135	salt … season salt was a preservative for meat; the sea hasn't enough to restore her name
137	attired wrapped up
139	belied falsely accused
149–50	given … fortune allowed matters to go on in this way
152	apparitions signs or fleeting appearances
159	with experimental seal together with my experience of life
159–60	warrant … book guarantees the truth of what my reading tells me
161	divinity status as a theologian
168	proper nakedness naked truth
176	change exchange
179	have the very bent are wholly disposed to
182	spirits toil … villainy whose energy is devoted to plotting
189	reft bereft of, robbed
193	quit me … throughly to be thoroughly even with them
198	a mourning ostentation all the appearance of mourning
206	on this travail from this labour
211	prize not to the worth do not fully appreciate
213	rack stretch to the utmost
218	study of imagination introspective brooding
220	in more precious habit more richly adorned
221	moving-delicate touchingly graceful
224	liver considered source of love and passion
227–9	doubt … likelihood follow my advice and things will turn out better than foreseen
230	levelled directed
233	sort not does not turn out

238	**inwardness** close attachment
242	**Being that … grief** since I am overwhelmed with grief
245	**to strange … cure** desperate diseases require desperate remedies
253–4	**right her** prove her innocent
256	**even** straightforward
266	**swear and eat it** swear and have to eat your words, i.e., deny your oath
270	**protest** swear or object
293	**bear her in hand** lead her on
294	**unmitigated rancour** uncontrolled hatred
297	**a proper saying** a likely story
301–2	**goodly count** sarcastic – a fine accusation
305	**trim** smooth, insincere
305–6	**as valiant … swears it** mere words establish a reputation for valour; no one asks for deeds
314–15	**render me … account** pay dearly for what he has done

CHECK THE BOOK

See Pamela Mason, 1992, for different interpretations of Beatrice in this scene, whether young and light-hearted, or mature and bitter. (See **Further reading**.)

SCENE 2

- Dogberry and associates interrogate Borachio and Conrade.
- They are taken to Leonato.

In prison, Dogberry, with the help of Verges and the sexton, interrogates Conrade and Borachio. In spite of Dogberry's ineptitude, the sexton appreciates the importance of the testimony and orders the prisoners to be taken to Leonato. Before they leave, Conrade pronounces Dogberry an ass, causing great offence and provoking a spirited defence of his dignity.

COMMENTARY

The sexton appears only in this scene. He gives the trial some legitimacy and contrasts comically with the bumbling constables.

The comedy is touchingly **ironic** and farcical. Dogberry asks, meaning assembly, 'Is our whole dissembly appeared' (line 1), unwittingly speaking the truth – it is a perversion of an assembly. He answers the sexton's, 'Which be the malefactors?' (line 3) confidently, 'Marry, that am I and my partner' (line 4), and funnily: they are literally malefactors, making a mess of the interrogation. It is even funnier when the irrepressible Verges confirms Dogberry's words with the nonsensical, 'we have the exhibition to examine' (line 5).

Dazzled and inflated by ordering information written down when he himself cannot write, Dogberry makes himself ridiculous by recording the least important facts. His lack of authority and vacuousness burlesque the harsh inquisitor. Yet his sincere indignation is touching and his climactic **malapropism**, 'everlasting redemption' (lines 47–8), meaning damnation, elicits kindly laughter. Nettled by Dogberry's overbearing self-importance, Conrade calls him an ass, which raises Dogberry's indignation to a ridiculous peak 'Oh that I had been writ down an ass!' (lines 70–1) he reiterates, ironically etching the fact on the audience's consciousness not as preposterous but true. When he asks, meaning respect, 'Does not thou suspect my place? Dost thou not suspect my years' (line 61), his last shred of dignity deserts him.

Dogberry's reasonable self justification has an underlying pathos. He may not be but he has a right to think of himself as a 'wise fellow'. He is indeed 'an officer', 'a householder', 'a rich fellow enough … that hath had losses … that hath two gowns, and everything handsome about him'. His pride and his self respect are as commendable as his boast that he knows the law and is a 'pretty piece of flesh' are ridiculous (lines 65–70).

This sentimental comedy contrasts with the comedy of wit and provides comic relief from Benedick's vow to challenge Claudio.

 **QUESTION**

Can you find any dignity in Dogberry's comic portrayal in this scene?

GLOSSARY		
1	**dissembly appeared** (malapropism) assembly; are we all here?	
5	**exhibition** (malapropism) commission (from Leonato)	

15	we hope we believe so
19	it ... shortly it will soon be generally believed to be so
22–3	go about with him deal with, i.e., outsmart him
24	false knaves rogues, unintentionally equivocal
26	in a tale telling the same story
28	go not ... examine you are not examining them properly
30	eftest aptest and deftest combined in a new word
37	promise warn
42	**Flat burglary** downright theft – of Hero's life – although he must mean perjury
48	**redemption** (malapropism) perdition
56	**opinioned** (malapropism) pinioned or bound
59	**naughty** stronger than now – worthless, wicked
59	**varlet** rogue
61	**suspect my place** (malapropism) respect my position
61–2	**suspect my years** he does, **ironically**, if years could mean ears, like a donkey's
64	**piety** (malapropism) impiety or irreverence
68	**go too** I'll have you know
70–1	**oh that I ... ass** that I could have been recorded as an ass (in writing); he has, for ever!

CONTEXT

In Messina, even the comic characters are preoccupied with status and honour, possibly a reflection of prejudice about Italy.

ACT V

SCENE 1

- After much ill-feeling between Leonato, Don Pedro and Claudio, Hero's innocence is established.
- To make amends Claudio agrees to marry Antonio's daughter, sight unseen.

CHECK THE BOOK

John Turner, 'Claudio and the code of honour', identifies the setting as 'late fourteenth century Sicily under the rule of the Spanish kings of Aragon; and its central interest is the code of honour by which the rule was maintained', Cookson and Loughrey, 1989, p. 23.

Antonio tries to comfort Leonato, who is inconsolable and beginning to suspect that Hero has been falsely accused. When Don Pedro and Claudio appear, Leonato flares up, accusing Claudio of having slandered Hero and challenging him to a duel. Antonio flies into a rage and also challenges Claudio, who disdainfully refuses both. The old men leave and Benedick arrives. Claudio makes callous jokes. Benedick remains serious and challenges him. The constables enter with Conrade and Borachio under arrest. Don Pedro and Claudio learn that they were mistaken, which they apologise for to Leonato, who has returned. They agree to proclaim to the people of Messina Hero's innocence and to sing hymns at her tomb. Claudio further agrees to make amends by marrying Antonio's daughter, sight unseen, who will be Hero disguised.

COMMENTARY

This resembles the denunciation scene (IV.1): loose in structure and episodic, it alternates the comic and serious. Except for the Friar, Leonato has the longest verse speech when he complains inconsolably that only a person in precisely his situation could understand and feel as he feels. The length, complex structure and elaborate imagery define Leonato's character:

> men
> Can counsel and speak comfort to that grief,
> Which they themselves not feel, but tasting it,
> Their counsel turns to passion, which before,
> Would give preceptial medicine to rage,
> Fetter strong madness in a silken thread,
> Charm ache with air, and agony with words. (lines 20–26)

CONTEXT

Leonato and Antonio conform to the stereotype of feeble old men in Italian and Elizabethan comedy.

Sententious and verbose, he repeats himself and struggles to come to the point, a stereotypical old man, impotent in his rage. Patience and counsel he cites several times, uses **synonyms** for measure to communicate the immeasurability of his woe and having scorned the consolation of 'proverbs' (line 17) and 'preceptial medicine' (line 24) he sums up his own argument with an **aphorism** which renders the thirty preceding lines superfluous: 'For there was never yet philosopher / That could endure the tooth-ache patiently' (lines 35–6).

The scene degenerates into predictable and sentimental farce when the brother who had counselled patience tries to goad Claudio into a sword fight. Although Claudio and Don Pedro maintain their composure, acting with just and dignified respect to old men, they look ridiculous and callous.

When Benedick enters, sympathy for his friends vanishes in their wisecracks and insults to Leonato and Antonio so soon after Hero's supposed death. Their pride inflates just before a fall too low, according to some readers, for Claudio ever to rise again. His dismissive, 'We had like to have our noses snapped off with two old men without teeth' (lines 112–13) and Don Pedro's arrogant, 'I doubt we should have been too young for them' (line 115), fall flat. It takes several curt retorts and a long speech aside to Claudio before he registers that Benedick is in earnest – Benedick whose transformation from mocker to woman's champion ennobles him. His parting, 'I will leave you to your gossip-like humour' (lines 167–8) **ironically** measures his moral growth and distances him from his friends.

> **CONTEXT**
>
> Irony and self-deception lighten what might have been a serious challenge.

Even after Don John's plot is exposed, they make arrogant fun of Dogberry and Verges. Thus their shame is sudden and absolute. Don Pedro's 'Runs not this speech like iron through your blood?' (line 214) communicates his mortification rhetorically and Claudio's, whose apostrophe, 'Sweet Hero! now thy image doth appear / In the rare semblance that I loved it first' (lines 219–20), ironically echoes his condemnation of the 'sign and semblance of her honour' (IV.1.28). By requesting a penance and agreeing to marry a fictitious unseen cousin, a double heiress, Claudio takes steps towards redemption. Leonato's forgiveness is immediately noble and generous.

 QUESTION

Is Claudio irredeemably callous or merely forgivably naïve?

Dogberry's ridiculous intervention increases the momentum of the movement towards a happy ending. His, 'masters, do not forget to specify when time and place shall serve, that I am an ass' (lines 223–4), ensures that we shall not. His warning about the machinations of the villainous Deformed pokes fun at vulgar superstition about the devil and comments **satirically** on the incarnate power of evil in the world. His farewells are a comic *tour de force* in their disorder and their insulting overtones.

> **CONTEXT**
>
> An Elizabethan audience would have taken Dogberry's references to the devil more literally than a modern audience.

QUESTION

'The tragic undertones of *Much Ado About Nothing* undermine the romantic comedy and bring into prominence the complexity and difficulty of human relationships.' Consider your response to the play in the light of this view.

GLOSSARY

7	**suit with** match
12	**answer every ... strain** correspond pang for pang
14	**lineament, branch** feature, limb
16	**And sorrow ... hem** drive grief away by croaking out platitudes
17	**Patch grief with proverbs** patch over wounds of grief with moral tags
17–18	**make ... candle-wasters** drown sorrow in philosophy
24	**Would give ... rage** would prescribe moral sentences for those in the throes of fury
25	**Fetter strong ... thread** try to shackle violent rage with thin thread
26	**Charm ache** control pain
28	**wring** struggle
32	**advertisement** good advice, instruction
38	**made a push ... sufferance** scoffed at misfortune and suffering
51	**If he could right ... lie low** If he could make himself better by quarrelling, we would have to watch out
58	**fleer** sneer or gibe
59	**dotard** senile old man
60	**As under ... age** not hiding behind my great age
62	**to thy head** in absolute defiance
66	**trial of a man** single combat
70	**never scandal slept** never before has scandal been buried
75	**nice fence** skilful swordsmanship
76	**bloom of lustihood** full-bloomed vigour
78	**daff me** put me aside
84	**foining fence** parrying sword play, not fighting in earnest
90	**apes** fools
90	**Jacks** rogues
92	**scruple** tiniest amount
93	**Scambling, out-facing, fashion-monging** argumentative, impudent, prettified
94	**cog** cheat
95	**Go anticly** walk in a grotesque manner, like a buffoon

118–19	**high proof** in the highest degree
129	**in the career** at full charge
131	**staff** lance-shaft
131	**broke cross** shattered by hitting his opponent at a glancing angle
134	**how ... girdle** what to do about it
143–5	**calf, capon, woodcock** all stupid animals
144	**curiously** skilfully
151	**wise gentleman** (ironic), a fool
151	**hath the tongues** speaks several languages
153	**forswore** took back, retracted
154	**trans-shape** distort
159	**deadly** until she dies
161–2	**God ... garden** (biblical) reference to Benedick's deception
168	**gossip-like humour** the humour of gossiping old women
179	**pretty** (ironic) fine
179–80	**doublet and hose** ordinary clothes
181	**giant/ ape/ doctor** hero / fool/ wise man
185–6	**ne'er weigh ... balance** never again weigh up the evidence in her scales
186–7	**cursing hypocrite** lying impostor
189	**Hearken after** inquire into
193–4	**verified unjust things** (malapropism) told lies
198	**in his own division** divide up in his own way
199	**there's ... suited** eloquently expressed; you've found four ways of saying the same thing
200–1	**bound to your answer** tied up, required to answer charges; answer: both reply and punishment for crime
221	**rare semblance** exquisite appearance
232	**beliest thyself** wrong yourself
240	**Impose ... penance** make me suffer whatever punishment
245	**enjoin** commit
250	**labour aught** perform any service
258	**Give her the right** marry her
261–2	**dispose ... of** from now on do what you like with

continued

QUESTION

Claudio has been condemned as a superficial fortune-hunter, unworthy of Hero. Do you agree with this view?

Scene 1 continued

266	**packed** involved
270	**by her** about her
271	**under white and black** in writing
283	**foundation** he gives thanks as if having received alms at a religious foundation
291	**look for you** expect you
294	**lewd** base, worthless

SCENE 2

- There is a happy interlude of banter between Benedick and Margaret and Benedick and Beatrice.
- Don John's plot is uncovered.

Benedick encounters Margaret in the orchard for a merry, bawdy skirmish of wit before sending her to fetch Beatrice. He belabours a love poem until she arrives. Having informed her that he has challenged Claudio, he and Beatrice mock each other playfully until Ursula enters to tell them that Don John's plot is uncovered and they leave happily to get the full story.

COMMENTARY

This scene is an interlude showing Beatrice's and Benedick's ease and happiness with each other and the superiority of an honest relationship based on mutual respect.

Margaret unleashes a string of *double-entendres* at Benedick: 'To have no man come over me' (line 6); 'Give us the swords, we have bucklers of our own' (line 13). His retort, 'You must put in the pikes with a vice' (line 14), though witty, lacks the edge of his conflict with Beatrice.

 QUESTION

Is the resumption of bawdy wit with Margaret and verbal sparring with Beatrice a sign that conflict between the sexes is inevitable?

The subsequent dialogue with Beatrice is typically barbed, yet candid. Benedick concludes, 'Thou and I are too wise to woo peaceably' (line 54), and Beatrice concurs: to be true to themselves, some antagonism must remain. The self-deprecating **bathos** of his exit lines is of a man at ease with himself, the woman he loves and the world: 'I will live in thy heart, die in thy lap, and be buried in thy eyes; and moreover, I will go with thee to thy uncle's' (lines 78–9).

GLOSSARY	
1	deserve ... hands earn my gratitude
2	helping ... speech getting me the chance to talk to
4	style (pun) stile
12	give thee the bucklers throw down shield to acknowledge defeat
13	bucklers / swords doubles-entendres for the female belly and male sexual organs
14	pikes central spikes in shields, a phallic symbol
15	vices bawdy – thighs closed in sexual intercourse
23	Leander legendary faithful lover who swam the Hellespont to visit his Hero
24	Troilus ... pandars wooed Cressida through Pandarus
25	quondam carpet-mongers former frequenters of ladies' bedrooms
31	in festival terms in the style of public display, i.e., in poetry
36	that I came what I came for – to hear the challenge
43–4	subscribe him proclaim or write him down as
46	so politic a state such a well-organised rule
51–2	spite it trouble it
55–6	there's not ... himself self-praise is no recommendation
57	instance proverb
57–8	time of good neighbours not now
62	clamour ... rheum noise of funeral bell and widow's weeping
63	Don Worm conscience
73	yonder's old coil there's a fine old rumpus at home
78	die in thy lap innuendo for sexual intercourse

SCENE 3

- At Hero's tomb Claudio and Don Pedro mourn her publicly.
- They leave to prepare for the wedding.

CONTEXT

In *Romeo and Juliet* the lovers' supposed deaths have tragic consequences whereas here the comedy is maintained.

Before dawn the next morning at Hero's empty tomb Claudio and Don Pedro make a public show of grief. Claudio recites an epitaph and a song of apology is sung. As dawn breaks, Claudio and Don Pedro leave to change their clothes for the wedding.

COMMENTARY

This is a brief scene of pomp, ceremony and dignified atonement. The song explores the destructive male inconstancy of 'Sigh no more' (II.3). When Don Pedro notes the first glimmer of daylight he speaks **metaphorically** of the 'wolves' of jealousy and villainy which have 'preyed' (line 25) in the night of human irrationality or sin; the gentle day of love and reason returns. **Blank verse**, classical allusion and formal syntax lend the utterance dignity and establish a new order: 'the gentle day, / Before the wheels of Phoebus, round about / Dapples the drowsy east with spots of grey' (lines 25–7). **Alliteration**, assonance of short vowel sounds and rhythm create appropriate lightness of tone.

GLOSSARY	
5	**guerdon** recompense
12	**goddess of the night** Cynthia, goddess of the moon and patroness of virgins
13	**thy virgin knight** Hero as knight errant, warring huntress
26	**Phoebus** Apollo, sun god, who drives his chariot across the sky
29	**several** separate
30	**weeds** clothes
32	**Hymen** god of marriage

SCENE 4

- At the wedding Antonio's daughter turns out to be none other than Hero.
- Benedick and Beatrice are betrothed.
- Don John is captured.

Waiting in his house for the ceremony to begin, Leonato grants Benedick's request to marry Beatrice. Don Pedro arrives with Claudio, who weds Hero, masked as Antonio's daughter. Hero unveils to his joyful surprise. After some sparring, Beatrice agrees to marry Benedick. A messenger bears the news of Don John's capture. Benedick urges Don Pedro to marry and orders the musicians to strike up for a dance.

COMMENTARY

As he asks for Beatrice's hand, Benedick exuberantly mocks himself as a lover. For a misogynist to marry is 'To bind me or undo me' (line 20). Not until the end of the scene is there a hint that he knows he was tricked into loving Beatrice.

His earthy, realistic love contrasts with Claudio's. He puns on the phallic connotations of will, hoping that Leonato's 'good will' may 'stand with ours' (lines 28–9). Marriage is an acknowledgement that 'the world must be peopled' (II.3.197); only an equal in wit and energy would tie Benedick down happily.

Beatrice and Benedick have the last say. After the solemnity of the wedding of Claudio and Hero, with its hint of miracle, it is a coming down to earth. Had either had an excess of pride or vanity, the disclosure that neither loves the other any 'more than reason' (line 74) would have been destructive. Their 'no more [love] than reason' could be played as a challenge, with tongue in cheek or as another joke gone wrong. When Claudio and Hero supply written proof of their feelings, there is relief that their marriage will be consummated.

> **CONTEXT**
>
> Even in Gielgud's fantastic 1949 production, the seriousness or Claudio's rejection of Hero and reconciliation with her were brought out through a realistic church setting.

CHECK THE BOOK

See Carol Neely, Harold Bloom, ed., 1988, pp. 120–121 for a disapproving view of Hero's and Beatrice's marital fates.

Benedick's 'I take thee for pity' (line 92) and Beatrice's, 'I yield upon great persuasion, and partly to save your life' (line 93), cast an **ironic**, self-mocking glance back at their former disdain and promise the audience that the 'merry war' (I.1.45) will continue beyond the altar.

With 'Peace! I will stop your mouth' (line 96), unless, as early texts suggest, Leonato speaks the line and thrusts Beatrice towards him, Benedick silences her with a kiss. Beatrice remains silent, whether deferring to her groom, or mortified at the coercion, or content with male domination, sexual frustration the cause of all her wit and scorn. Feminists may take exception to the kiss, fearing that Beatrice has conformed like Hero. Yet Beatrice was gleeful before the kiss, neither do we doubt that the merry war will continue, and Benedick is elated not by domination but mutual respect and support: 'a college of wit-crackers cannot flout me out of my humour … never flout at me for what I have said against it' (line 98); 'get thee a wife! There is no staff more reverend than one tipped with horn!' (line 115). Nothing is hidden. He acknowledges what he was and proclaims without shame what he now is. He has not abandoned his bawdy wit, he continues to indulge in rhetorical exaggeration and he still refers to cuckoldry, but with self-mockery.

Benedick is reconciled with Claudio, which furthers his redemption. Claudio flatters Benedick with a teasing story of Jove visiting Europa as a bull. Benedick's retort, harping on Claudio's youth and feebleness, reestablishes normal relations. This is strengthened after the ceremony when Benedick 'did think to have beaten thee' (line 105) and Claudio 'might have cudgelled thee out of thy single life' (line 108), which are innocuous, playful threats.

Don Pedro and Claudio remain arrogant and insensitive to the end. Claudio flatters himself that he has done the decent thing in marrying sight unseen an heiress whose wealth is her only commendation. His boast, 'I'll hold my mind were she an Ethiop' (line 38) strengthens the argument that he remains a callow materialist (his youth always the only excuse), in spite of his penance.

Hero presents her unveiling as a miracle: 'when I lived, I was your other wife'. She has risen from the dead, 'One Hero died defiled, but I do live …' (line 63). Claudio has regained his virgin, plus something indefinable, whether the undeserved and unexpected gift of unqualified forgiveness or the addition of self-knowledge through suffering. The Friar's intervention hints at the mysterious goodness of providence. Dissatisfaction may remain that Hero should offer no reproach and has to be doubly pure to be an acceptable reward for a man himself so flawed.

Overall, however, the ending depicts harmonious reconciliation, symbolised by the music and dance which draws the curtain down. Normality, enhanced by the union of two couples and the certainty that life is to be perpetuated, has been reestablished.

QUESTION

Are the darker undertones dispelled at the end of the play?

EXTENDED COMMENTARIES

TEXT 1 CLAUDIO'S DENUNCIATION OF HERO (IV.1.1–56)

LEONATO:
Come, Friar Francis, be brief, only to the plain form of marriage, and you shall recount their particular duties afterwards.

…

HERO:
Is my lord well, that he doth speak so wide?

Anticipation does not blunt the shocking dramatic impact of Claudio's denunciation: he had already vowed to 'shame' (III.2.92) Hero publicly, with Don Pedro's backing. His 'Give not this rotten orange to your friend' (IV.1.27), insulting to Hero and Leonato, was also anticipated – by Beatrice's perceptive comment, at the masked ball, that he was 'civil as an orange' and 'of that jealous complexion' (II.1.223). Claudio's undeserved insult is harsh, whether he hands Hero coldly back to Leonato or, as in some productions, flings her brutally to the ground.

Claudio's gradual takeover of the ceremony and his rising fury against both Hero and Leonato, so fussily impatient to expedite the marriage service, create tension and pathos. Claudio's blunt, unexpected 'No' (line 4) to the friar's perfunctory question exudes malice. When he twists Leonato's embarrassed, 'I dare make his answer' (line 13), with the menacing bombast of, 'What men daily do, not knowing what they do!' (lines 14–15), he deflects his anger from Hero, whom he cannot face or name, on to her unsuspecting father. Deferring his accusation strengthens its eventual impact. Benedick's attempt to lighten the atmosphere, 'Interjections?' (line 16) foreshadows his defection from his comrades and alliance with Beatrice.

Claudio's 'Stand thee by' (line 18) to the friar and transition to **blank verse** signals the collapse of wedding ceremony into denunciation ritual. Leonato's pathetically appeasing, 'son' (line 21) is met with sarcasm, 'What have I to give you back, whose worth / May counterpoise this rich and precious gift?' (line 23), echoing bitterly his earlier idealisation of Hero as a jewel. In patriarchal Messina as man's property, Hero was about to be transferred from father to husband. Although the imagery elevated her virginal purity, silence reduced her to an object of male honour. Don Pedro cues Claudio with 'unless you render her again' (line 24), which is ignoble and spiteful. Since she is pure, an unsettling **irony** tinges the entire denunciation. Claudio's rhetorical use of exclamations, interrogatives, **hyperbole** and anticlimax creates melodrama, indicative of youthful inexperience and a straining after effect ironically reinforcing her innocence. He had attributed bewitching power to beauty at the masked ball. Now he declaims, 'Oh what authority and show of truth / Can cunning sin cover itself withal!' (line 30–1). Like Benedick, he fears female sexuality, which the enshrinement of male honour and female virginity purports to control. 'Would you not swear', he demands, 'that she were a maid' (lines 33–4), expressing the insecurity of Messina's men, who insist upon the privilege of dictating female behaviour. Ironically her 'exterior shows' (line 35) do reflect her inner worth, her dishonour his fear.

Leonato, pathetically confused, expresses his willingness to overlook the fault if Claudio and Hero are already lovers. The quiet dignity of Hero's protest and appeal to reason deepens the **pathos**.

CHECK THE BOOK

Joseph Westlund argues sympathetically that Claudio's 'idealisation and degradation are defences against anxiety caused by sexual impulses' in his psychoanalytic essay, 'The Temptation to Isolate', Harold Bloom, ed., 1988, pp. 63–70.

Unmoved, Claudio adopts an elevated classical image of 'Diana in her orb, / As chaste as is the bud ere it be blown' to contrast with 'Venus', 'intemperate in your blood' (lines 51–3) and represent his horror at Hero's sensuality and hypocrisy. Ironically these extremes mask Hero's reality. He explodes with the insult, 'approved wanton' to which Don Pedro adds, 'common stale' (line 59), both learned from the bastard, Don John, symbol of their baser nature.

This climactic ado has arisen from nothing but a malign deception, unlike the love-creating benign deceptions of Beatrice and Benedick. It dramatises the theme of male inconstancy of Balthasar's song, since Claudio disparages whom he once exalted. The masked ball and wedding point to the blind irrationality and subjectivity of love. Spying, eavesdropping, misreporting and deception suggest that a rigidly hierarchical society stultifies feelings and suppresses truth. The denunciation scene crystallises these themes and anticipates the emergence of Beatrice's and Benedick's more realistic and antagonistic love.

 **CHECK THE BOOK**

A. C. Swinburne, in John Russell Brown, ed., 1979, regarded the marriage of Hero and Claudio as 'a doubtfully desirable consummation', p. 40.

TEXT 2 BEATRICE AND BENEDICK REVEAL THEIR LOVE FOR EACH OTHER (IV.1.248–316)

BENEDICK:
Lady Beatrice, have you wept all this while?

...

BENEDICK:
Enough, I am engaged, I will challenge him. I will kiss your hand, and so I leave you: by this hand, Claudio shall render me a dear account: as you hear of me, so think of me: go comfort your cousin, I must say she is dead, and so farewell.

Benedick dramatically breaches male solidarity, anticipated by his **ironic** interjections during the denunciation, by staying behind to comfort weeping Beatrice. We anticipate comic relief after Hero's ordeal from Beatrice's and Benedick's embarrassment – the scorners of love, in love and alone together.

The sincere simplicity of 'Lady Beatrice, have you wept all this while?' (line 248) resonates with his opening insult, 'What, my dear

Lady Disdain! Are you yet living?' (I.1.88). Claudio's engagement had weakened Benedick's misogynist stance. As Beatrice's position was always precarious – dependent and subservient to her young, marriageable cousin – pathos suffuses their exchanges.

Her hint for him to leave, 'I will weep a little while longer' (line 249), is coy. Asserting that Hero 'is wronged' (line 252) he becomes her ally. With subtle verbal fencing she gauges her influence over him. By regretting that there is no man to defend Hero, she paves his way to a full declaration: 'I do love nothing in the world so well as you, is not that strange?' (lines 259–60). The first clause is conventional romantic **hyperbole**, which the rhetorical question of the second half makes sincere. He reminds Beatrice, and the audience, how unexpected such a proposal from such a misogynist is. Characteristically detached when he comments ironically on life, he invites a disclosure from Beatrice by admitting the foreignness and transformative power of love.

Comically unwilling to relinquish her advantage, she stumbles over words, equivocates and retracts, not yielding too cheaply, which he sees through and swears, 'By my sword' (line 265), that she loves him. She ridicules his gallantry, 'Do not swear and eat it' (line 266). Each so enjoys parodying the language of courtly love that merry war almost resumes, until she concedes, 'I was about to protest I loved you' (lines 273–4) – past tense and still oblique – before the dramatically unequivocal, 'I love you with so much of my heart, that nothing is left to protest' (lines 276–7) a generous gesture from a professed man-hater.

QUESTION

To what extent does the strength of the 'Kill Claudio!' and other comic scenes lie in rapid reversals of thought and mood?

Parodying the conventionally grateful lover – 'Come bid me do anything for thee' (line 279) – Benedick offers to translate sincerity into action. Lines are short, their tone edgy, each using wit to mask feeling. Beatrice's 'Kill Claudio!' (line 279), blunt and shocking, dispels romance and returns to Hero's tragedy and Benedick's comic discomfort. Beatrice's line is pivotal to any interpretation of her character, whether hissed with the shrew's aggression or muttered through the clenched teeth of a spinster's insecurity.

Benedick's reply, 'Ha, not for the wide world' (line 280), comically contradicts his earlier pledge. The speeches become longer and faster as Beatrice convinces Benedick to call Claudio to account. Torn between tenderness for Benedick and pity for Hero her emotions erupt. She repeats, blatantly manipulatively, with comic incongruity in a love scene, 'Oh that I were a man' (line 292). Having 'slandered, scorned, dishonoured' Hero with 'unmitigated rancour' (line 294), Claudio represents despised 'manhood … melted into curtsies, valour into compliment' (line 304). She had vowed never to marry a 'piece of valiant dust' (II.1.44) – a man – to become the passive, submissive Messina wife. Her desire to 'eat his heart in the market place' (IV.1.295) is disturbing: does her contempt for civilised man originate in a perverse attraction to virile savagery or does she exaggerate to shame Benedick into avenging Hero? 'Use it for my love some other way than swearing it' (line 309) elicits active commitment, not empty profession.

Benedick's submission to female aggression is a comic reversal. He had begun idealising bachelor freedom the moment Claudio pledged himself to Hero. The bond Beatrice so passionately proposes is kinder and more heartfelt than male solidarity. She domesticates honour and exposes the emptiness of male valour. In everyday service to justice he will achieve a fuller manhood than his legendary heroes. His comic detachment will yield to action and her frustrated will achieve satisfaction. For Benedick, whose wit is childishly whimsical and self-indulgent, being dominated is comic but entirely appropriate.

Text 3 Benedick challenges Claudio to a duel (v.1.109–174)

CLAUDIO:
Now, signor, what news?

…

DON PEDRO:
He is in earnest.

The audience share Benedick's awkwardness as he enters, pledged to avenge Hero's dishonour, just after Claudio and Don Pedro, oblivious to his intentions, have fended off Leonato and Antonio.

QUESTION

How satisfying do you find the union of Beatrice and Benedick at the end of *Much Ado About Nothing,* and what does the play suggest about human love?

Benedick ignores Claudio's familiar 'what news' (line 109) to address Don Pedro more formally, 'Good day, my lord' (line 109). Tension increases when Benedick ignores Claudio's callously disrespectful reference to 'two old men without teeth' (lines 112–13) whose daughter and niece he has dishonoured and, he believes, killed. His former deference to Leonato now appears as shallow self-interest. Don Pedro boasts, 'we should have been too young for them' (line 115), which alienates him from the audience who sense Benedick's growing unease as his antagonism and commitment to Hero's vindication go unrecognised.

CHECK THE BOOK

Pamela Mason, 1992, argues that Claudio's refusal to take Benedick's challenge seriously is a further sign of 'the insistent theatricality of a narcissistic society', p. 17.

Benedick attempts to antagonise and alienate Claudio and Don Pedro with his proverbial 'in a false quarrel there is no true valour' and baldly impersonal 'I came to seek you both' (lines 116–17). Claudio remains impervious, even after Benedick acknowledges him by offering to draw his sword. Faced with cold silence or stiff retorts, he has jested, either to cover up inner turmoil or from youthful callousness. Don Pedro interprets Benedick's pallor as either anger or illness. The expected confrontation is delayed when Claudio deduces that Benedick's mood has nothing to do with him. Still Benedick does not affront Claudio openly, adopting a jousting **metaphor**, to which Claudio responds verbally without seeing its aggressive intent. As the audience and now Don Pedro know what Benedick is feeling, Claudio's persistent blindness screws up the tension and makes him seem unusually undiscerning. Don Pedro's comment tells the audience that Benedick's gestures and manner have made his anger increasingly transparent. Finally and dramatically, Claudio realises that Benedick is angry with him. Consistent with their former bonhomie, he responds by jokingly proposing to fight, boasting of his prowess, but in an inappropriately trifling tone that sounds like empty bravado. By taking Claudio aside and whispering in his ear in unadorned language – 'villain', 'cowardice', 'death shall fall heavy' (lines 137–40) – that underlines the human destruction Claudio's slander has caused, Benedick has created expectations of open conflict.

Don Pedro, whether to lighten the atmosphere or from insensitivity or disrespect for Leonato's household, teases Benedick about Beatrice in Benedick's renowned broadly witty style. As the audience sees the joking as out of place and arrogant, it highlights the change in Benedick that attachment to Beatrice has made in him. Reference to 'the old man's daughter' (line 159) is shockingly arrogant in its disrespect to Leonato and to the supposedly dead Hero. Thus Benedick has the audience's support when he insults Claudio's vaunted nobility and his manhood with 'your wit ambles well' (line 146). By changing the subject and making stale cuckold jokes, Claudio and Don Pedro, with ignoble trifling, avoid Benedick's challenge. His refusal to joke makes the second challenge, proclaimed not whispered, more dramatic, and with its slight on Claudio's youth, cowardice and effeminacy, less easily evaded. His insult to Don Pedro's baseness and cowardice, is superbly and, to the audience, triumphantly, understated beneath a pose of deference: 'my lord, for your many courtesies, I thank you: I must discontinue your company: your brother the bastard is fled from Messina: you have among you killed a sweet and innocent lady' (lines 169–172). 'Sweet' underlines Hero's innocence and magnifies the enormity of the slander. Respect for Benedick has grown as he makes known to former comrades his change of heart and disapproval of their conduct. Although Claudio and Don Pedro make fun of him for losing his temper and starting a fight, the last laugh is on them when they acknowledge that Don John's flight might indicate guilt.

CHECK THE NET

For information about the Royal Shakespeare Company, one of the finest theatre companies in the world, based in Stratford-upon-Avon, visit **http://www.rsc. org.uk**.

PART THREE

CRITICAL APPROACHES

CHARACTERISATION

The antagonism and attraction of the sexual battle between Beatrice and Benedick produces sharp repartee, droll, whimsical images and wonderfully versatile, thought-provoking wit. Claudio's language lacks wit and his behaviour is conventional; Hero is obedient and hardly speaks at all. The Beatrice–Benedick, Hero–Claudio plots resonate and interlink to create a vision of reconciliation and harmony through sexual love. It is sometimes argued that the Hero–Claudio plot would collapse on its own. However, their love story is the spine of the play, their eventual marriage its consummation. Beatrice's and Benedick's story arises from, depends upon and complements it. It was adapted from popular romances, whereas the subplot is the original product of Shakespeare's own imagination. Its quality of spontaneous improvisation creates spaciousness, freedom and exuberance. When independent characters scornful of romantic love succumb to feeble deceptions, the power of love as a universal solvent is exalted.

> **CONTEXT**
>
> Shakespeare adapted the Hero–Claudio plot but invented the Beatrice and Benedick plot.

BENEDICK

Benedick's name means he who is to be blessed, Beatrice's, she who blesses, which indicates that they were destined for each other. His prototypes are two stock characters of comedy: the scorner of love and the witty courtier. He has an **ironic** sense of himself; an actor plays Benedick who is conscious of playing himself. Don Pedro warns, proverbially, 'In time the savage bull doth bear the yoke', meaning that he must succumb to matrimony, to which Benedick retorts: 'The savage bull may; but if ever the sensible Benedick bear it, pluck off the bull's horns and set them in my forehead, and let me be vilely painted, and in such great letters as they write, "Here is good horse to hire", let them signify under my sign, "Here you may see Benedick, the married man"' (I.2.193–9). The quick retort to a stale proverb is one of his hallmarks, another his ability to conjure up cartoon images with words. The too audacious expression of pride, presaging his fall, and his anxiety about being made a cuckold are funny. Equally so is his childish self-dramatisation – his name mentioned twice in the third person – as a notorious scorner of woman and recognisable social type.

Asked by Claudio for his opinion of Hero, he had replied, 'Do you question me as an honest man … or would you have me speak after my custom, as being a professed tyrant to their sex?' (I.1.122–4). This is often cited as proof that misogyny is a pose adopted to protect him from women and amuse his friends; since it is a pose, his falling for Beatrice, it is argued, is no surprise. Yet a pose may be sincerely adopted and fully embraced, scorn of women no less genuine for its self-consciousness, the fear no less real for its self-dramatising playfulness.

Although his patronising of Claudio and the sophistication of his wit have prompted directors to cast Benedick as mature, verging on middle age, his fondness for painting fantastic, outlandish, whimsical cartoons and almost gloating over his comic self-image may reflect the immaturity of one little older than Claudio and just as susceptible to marriage.

This ironic attitude towards himself is apparent in major soliloquies where he weighs up the discrepancy between how the world sees him and he sees himself – after Beatrice dissects his masked character at the ball, in the garden before and after the eavesdropping and after Beatrice has entered to bid him come to dinner. Speaking to himself, he speaks of himself in a manner not far different from the Benedick who speaks to others. His openness about himself is engaging; his self-dramatisation arises from an insecurity about who he is, which makes him accessible.

Benedick exercises a fool's licence from the moment he interrupts a courtly exchange with his mischievous question about Hero's paternity, 'Were you in doubt, sir, that you asked her?' (I.1.79). His particular talent is not merely for wittily voicing disdain of romantic love; he is quick to deflate pomposity and undermine whoever takes his own shaky social *persona* too seriously. Though a professed woman-hater, he boasts that he is 'loved of all ladies' (I.1.92–3). only Beatrice excepted. He is a notorious womaniser, who dreads

CHECK THE NET

For useful discussion of character and themes, see **http:// www.sparknotes. com/shakespeare/** and explore the Much Ado link.

love, marriage and the inevitability of being cuckolded. Don Pedro makes bawdy reference to Benedick's amours in Venice (I.1) and when in the orchard he reviews the attractions of different qualities in women, he does it with a connoisseur's familiarity. His dislike is not of women but their threat to male freedom, privilege and honour.

The particular quality of his wit can be savoured in his longer speeches, as when he complains at the masked ball: 'She used me past the endurance of a block: an oak but with one green leaf on it, would have answered her' (II.1.181–2). He exaggerates and multiplies fantastic images until the picture becomes grotesque. From the answering block, he descends into whimsy: 'my very visor began to assume life and scold with her' (II.1.182–3). He returns to the block to picture himself as a target shot at by the army of her jests: 'she speaks poniards, and every word stabs' (lines 186–7). The stabbing pain of her invective leads him to conclude that 'if her breath were as terrible as her terminations … she would infect the north star' (lines 187–9), another mocking **hyperbole**. The north star being remote in space, he appropriates biblical and classical allusions – Adam, Hercules and Ate – remote in time and mythology, to communicate his preferred remoteness from her and her unsuitableness as a wife. These allusions spark off theological and religious images, the ludicrous idea that 'people sin on purpose' in order to go to hell and escape her on earth, to which she, like the devil, brings, in theological terms, 'all disquiet, horror and perturbation' (lines 195–6). He is a Renaissance man, as comfortable citing sacred and secular literature as imagery from nature, the army and the brothel. The pace and volume of his wit implies sharp indignation which the witty turning of accumulating images diffuses. The pleasure he takes in showing off his learned wit and drinking in applause outweighs the anger her humiliation of him has raised.

Although Benedick complains of the agitation Beatrice causes, it is evident that his disposition, as a soldier, is restless and that there is some latent affinity between them. A block of wood, unfeeling and immobile, was his image of degradation; elsewhere it is a target and a 'for sale' sign on a horse, the boredom of a Sunday yoked to a wife or a great thaw when the roads are blocked and there is nothing to do. He associates movement and wit with masculine power and

CHECK THE FILM

In the BBC and Branagh films Benedick is an energetic young man; in a 1968 production a jaded soldier.

freedom, which married domesticity would curtail and, by pinning him down, in his castration-fearing eyes, cut off his virility and make him susceptible to cuckolding.

What Beatrice says to his visor at the masked ball sows seeds of self-doubt – 'the prince's fool! Hah, it may be I go under that title because I am merry' (II.1.155–6) – which are watered, as his **soliloquy** in the garden reveals, by Claudio's betrothal: 'may I be so converted and see with these eyes? I cannot tell, I think not' (II.3.18–19). Overhearing Beatrice praised and himself praised and dispraised, completes the process: 'I hear how I am censured … I did never think to marry … A man loves the meat in his youth, that he cannot endure in his age … When I said I would die a bachelor, I did not think I should live till I were married' (II.3.184–98). With former certainties undermined, he twists what he had said and thought about himself to justify becoming a lover. In the soliloquy after Beatrice has fetched him to dinner he also twists her words to give him some hope that she may love him. If his public *persona* has been a comic fabrication in which he never quite believed, to switch roles from scorner of love to lover in earnest is no wrench. Alternatively, as he has associated love and marriage with emasculation, boredom and death, desperation at the loss of Claudio to marriage and of social approval induces him to be tricked into love. Beatrice is ideally suited to soothe his fear of stagnation, since she stirs him up, and of emasculation, since she herself has a male wit.

The domestic atmosphere of Messina which changes Claudio from soldier to lover acts as a catalyst upon Benedick, whose imagination is fired by the fear of female entrapment. 'Prove that ever I lose more blood with love than I will get again with drinking', he retorts to Don Pedro's hint that he will follow Claudio into matrimony, 'pick out mine eyes with a ballad-maker's pen and hang me up at the door at a brothel-house for the sign of blind Cupid' (I.1.185–8). The image is grotesque, gruesome as well as whimsically comic, arising from fear of isolation. The next image is similarly comic, fantastic, self-mocking, and violent, 'hang me in a bottle like a cat and shoot at me' (I.1.191), hinting at a fear of annihilation if left to the mercy of women. By the time he is sitting in the orchard, the tone has

CONTEXT

The mistaking in Benedick's falling with love with Beatrice is comic, in Hero's repudiation of Hero it is tragic as it is in *Othello* and *King Lear*.

turned to self-pity, the broad **antithesis** expressing a soldier's
bluntness: 'He was wont to speak plain and to the purpose, like an
honest man and a soldier, and now is he turned orthography, his
words are a very fantastical banquet, just so many strange dishes'
(II.3.15–17). The grotesque violence of his response to Balthasar's
singing just before his conversion, 'Is it not strange that sheep's guts
should hale souls out of men's bodies?' (II.3.50–1) is the
exaggeration of a man truly susceptible and already won.

In the soliloquy after the eavesdropping, his childlike eagerness is
comic: he is yielding to desire, but his reasons are sound enough –
pity for her suffering, admiration for her beauty of person and
character, a humble sense of his own inadequacy as a single man and
an acceptance at his age of the biological and social necessity of
marriage. 'Lady Beatrice', he enquires with respect and sympathy
after Hero's rejection at the altar, 'have you wept all this while?'
(IV.1.248). Love has softened his heart as it hardens Claudio's, and
deepened his understanding, as he dissociates himself from Claudio
and Don Pedro and identifies Don John as the architect of Hero's
disgrace. The way he broaches his feelings to Beatrice, 'I do love
nothing in the world so well as you – is it not strange?' (IV.1.
259–260), has a simple dignity, wonder and rare candour. The
rhetorical question at the end is in keeping with his constant
detachment from himself while showing how miraculous his
feelings seem to him. His disinterest and sincerity create intimacy
and invite Beatrice to confess her feelings, which, after gentle
prodding, she does. Adopting the conventional pose of the courtly
lover he enquires, 'Come bid me do anything for thee'. When she
shocks him with 'Kill Claudio', his immediate response comes from
his loyalty to male honour – 'Ha, not for the wide world'
(IV.1.278–80). The ensuing dialogue comically renews their merry
war and confirms the suspicion that beneath the veneer of courtly
sophistication, military toughness and witty sexual disdain,
Benedick is too simple, spontaneous and insecure to be a match for
Beatrice. And yet his loss is his gain, since he grows in moral stature
when he challenges Claudio and renounces Don Pedro. In his sexual
partnership with Beatrice he has discovered a unity of heart beside
which male alliances pale.

**CHECK
THE BOOK**

See Roger Sales,
1987, for a
discussion of
Benedick's moral
growth.

At the end of the play, Benedick and Claudio are married and their
friendship resumes its former bantering style: 'I did think to have
beaten thee, but, in that thou art like to be my kinsman, live
unbruised and love my cousin' (V.4.105–6). His playfulness remains
with Beatrice as well: 'Come, I will have thee, but by this light I
take thee for pity' (V.4. 91–2). Yet his celebration of his change of
heart is unconstrained: 'since I do purpose to marry, I will think
nothing to any purpose that the world can say against it; and
therefore never flout at me for what I have said against it' (V.4.
101–3) 'Get thee a wife' (V.4.115), he advises Don Pedro
enthusiastically. Beatrice and Benedick had hurt each other in a
merry war which contradicted their true feelings. Their love
surpasses Claudio's and Hero's in its wit, openness and emotional
and intellectual vitality. Benedick's justification for his change of
heart, apart from love, is 'man is a giddy thing' (V.4.103–4). Love is
a means of accepting and living with the constancy of change.
Appropriately the play ends not with Hero and Claudio whose
strict adherence to an unbending code temporarily fragmented their
relationship but with Beatrice and Benedick. Their contentiousness
and honesty about the volatility of their feelings assure us that
within the security of a permanently committed relationship, they
will be constantly testing, questioning and reaffirming a deep love.

QUESTION

Are you satisfied
that Benedick has
matured
sufficiently for
marriage?

BEATRICE

Beatrice, 'Lady Disdain' (I.1.88), suffers the humiliation of being
duped, in the pivotal comic reversal, into falling in love with the
man she has most ostentatiously disdained. A moment later,
Benedick, gratefully parodying the chivalrous lover, generously
offers to prove his love by doing whatever she desires 'Kill
Claudio' (IV.1.79) she replies simply, aggressively reacting to the
sacrifice of her freedom. When Benedick demurs, she passionately
denounces Claudio, outraged that a privileged male can slander an
innocent woman with impunity. She retains a lady-like composure:
love has not weakened her female solidarity or determination to win
the merry war. Her manipulative complaint that 'manhood is melted
into curtsies … men are only turned into tongues' (IV.1.303–6),
echoes the earlier 'would it not grieve a woman to be overmastered
with a piece of valiant dust' (II.1.43–5). Such disdain implies an ideal

of chivalry founded upon action not gesture or pretence, as Claudio's and Leonato's onslaught upon Hero is.

Her playful **hyperbole**, though subtler and more elegiac, is reminiscent of Benedick, whom she forces to choose between friendship and love, truth and dishonour. Killing Claudio is more than measure for measure, since Hero, dishonoured and reported dead, is alive. Her repeated cries of, 'Oh God that I were a man' to 'eat his heart in the market place' (IV.1. 294–5) imply a savage ideal of virility, which may explain, in a highly civilised, effete society, her remaining unmarried. Torn by grief at Hero's suffering and joy from Benedick's love, she gives voice to aggression which society has conditioned her to suppress. She is also seeking proof of Benedick's worthiness and love. Love is not for her, as it is for Claudio, playing roles, observing and enforcing conventions, but of unreserved fellow feeling and commitment. When Benedick temporises, she explodes, 'there is no love in you' (IV.1. 283): her lover must feel and avenge Hero's suffering. Having lamented the lack of real men of action, she scoffs when he protests love, 'Use it for my love some other way than swearing it' (IV.1.309).

Her 'Oh God that I were a man' is a heart-felt cry against undeserved male privilege and the subordination of women. Injustice spurs her wit. Her irruption into the play rivets attention with its enigmatic and scornful impertinence – 'I pray you, is Signor Mountanto returned from the wars or no?' (I.1.23). Her mocking nickname implies that he is a gross braggart, whose safety is nevertheless a concern, if only to renew their public quarrel. Later she attracts his attention with her insulting 'nobody marks you' (I.1.86–7) (except her, of course). Her skirmish with the messenger anticipates the 'Kill Claudio'(IV.1.79): she dissects and subjects each innocent statement to a torrent of invective until he surrenders – 'I will hold friends with you, lady' (I.1.66). She takes pride in her outspoken scorn, having interrupted her uncle and taken her verbal assault beyond what good manners would allow. Her wit is aggressive and inventive, exaggeration, as with Benedick, her favourite weapon: 'four of his five wits went halting off and now is the whole man governed with one' (I.1.58–60); 'He hath every month a new sworn brother' (I.1.53). She resents Benedick's

CONTEXT

In the Trevor Nunn production of *Much Ado* in 1968, Beatrice's shrill cry 'Kill Claudio' released all the pent-up frustration of her role as dependent woman.

inconstancy: he had 'lent' his heart to her and 'won' hers 'with false dice' (II.1.211–13) hinting at an earlier attachment Although she would not have him 'put her down', lest she 'should prove the mother of fools' (II.1.215–16), she accepts that he 'would win any woman in the world if a could get her good will' (II.1.11–13).

Their reputation as longstanding rivals in wit with a romantic history has led some directors to present Beatrice as an ageing shrew threatened with the frustration of perennial spinsterhood and Benedick as a rake running out of younger companions to corrupt. Such a Beatrice hates men for spurning her and is driven to love by desperation. Although the allusiveness of her wit implies wide experience and education, her polished composure maturity, she is diminished if her edge arises from weakness – frustration, desperation – rather than strength – intelligence, gaiety, imagination, justified impatience with an unequal society.

Her wit has youth, if only its eternal spirit. Before the masked ball, Leonato warns that her sharp tongue will repel potential husbands. She adapts the superstition that a woman dying unmarried leads apes into hell: 'So deliver I up my apes, and away to Saint Peter: for the heavens, he shows me where the bachelors sit, and there live we, as merry as the day is long' (II.1.35–7). This is witty, good-humoured and self-deprecating. Although she constantly mocks male vanity and conceit, Don Pedro finds her 'pleasant-spirited' (II.1.258) and Leonato praises her warmly: 'she is never sad, but when she sleeps, and not ever sad then … she hath often dreamed of unhappiness, and waked herself with laughing' (II.1. 259–62).

The nothing overheard in the orchard causes Beatrice's ado, alternately rhyming **iambic pentameter** foregrounding her change of heart:

> Stand I condemned for pride and scorn so much?
> Contempt, farewell, and maiden pride, adieu,
> No glory lives behind the back of such.
> And Benedick, love on, I will requite thee,
> Taming my wild heart to thy loving hand: (III.2.108–12)

QUESTION

For Beatrice is marriage a desirable or merely unavoidable option?

The verse, unlike the elaborate formality of the courtier's speech, has simplicity and directness, candour and sincerity. Holy matrimony she deems preferable to solitary pride and scorn. Humbled, she is willing to let her love for Benedick soften and guide her affections.

Fending off his kiss in V.2 until sure that he has challenged Claudio, she has the confident familiarity of a longstanding wife. He asks with playful self-deprecation, expecting an **ironic** reply, 'for which of my bad parts didst thou first fall in love with me' (V.2. 44–5). She tells him that all his parts are so equally bad that she could not discriminate, before facetiously inquiring, 'for which of my good parts didst thou first suffer love for me?' (V.2.48). 'A good epithet' is Benedick's comment on 'suffer love'. She teases him, warmly and playfully, for his reluctance to love. They are 'too wise to woo peaceably' (V.2.54) which pleases her: antagonism will keep them in touch with their feelings.

A more shrewish or more doctrinaire feminist would be more averse to marriage. Her response to Benedick's, 'Do you not love me?' (V.4.73) at the end of the play is a reprise of Lady Disdain. Her 'I yield upon great persuasion, and partly to save your life, for I was told you were in a consumption' (lines 93–5) is a fair but witty retort to his jesting, 'I take thee for pity' (line 92); underlying both is sincere attachment and frankness.

With, 'Peace, I will stop thy mouth' (line 96), Benedick comically silences Beatrice: unable to outdo her verbally, he has resorted to force. There are unpleasant connotations – that Beatrice's wit was an outlet for repressed sexuality, that she uses it to get attention and ultimately domination by men. However, since Beatrice had urged Hero to stop Claudio's mouth with a kiss after his proposal, she could hardly object to being silenced in the same way. Yet she had trivialised the pattern of sexual relations, 'wooing, wedding, and repenting' (II.1.52–4) by comparing them with three sorts of dances, which, prophetically, Hero had to dance out before marriage.

The shallow hoax that changes Beatrice points to a deeper desire which love has released and fulfilled. As Benedick puts it, 'Man is a

CHECK THE BOOK

Carol Neely, Harold Bloom, ed., 1988, p. 112, argues that Beatrice is ambivalent about marriage.

giddy thing' (V.2.104), composed of flesh and spirit, powerless over destiny, subject to change, fated to die. He and Beatrice challenge conventions with their wit, their loyalty to their feelings and their capacity for change. Although socially Beatrice may be condemned to dance out the marriage measure she so cynically portrayed, in her heart and spirit she has the joy to transcend it.

CLAUDIO

Extreme shyness and reticence underline Claudio's and Hero's conventionality. Their rigidly hierarchical society exacts from its youth mercenary circumspection and romantic idealisation as preconditions to courtship and marriage. Hero's beauty and the romantic ideal of love strike Claudio dumb until he is left alone with Benedick. 'Can the world buy such a jewel?' he asks before proclaiming that 'she is the sweetest lady that ever I looked on' and promising, 'I would scarce trust myself … if Hero would be my wife' (I.1.134 & 144–5). The suddenness of his fall and its under-lying illusions are stressed by Benedick's cynically deflating replies and comments. Such romantic idealisation and reticence are the badge of youth. He had brought tears to his uncle's eyes by doing 'in the figure of a lamb the feats of a lion' (I.1.12). Claudio aspires to succeed on Messina's terms. Dreams of glory and heroism having spurred him to military renown and the patronage of Don Pedro; in peace Hero is the trophy worthy of his noble vision of his destiny.

Ambition makes him constantly deferential to Don Pedro, his patron, but capable of bantering with Benedick. He makes sure that Hero is an heiress before telling Don Pedro that he is in earnest. Often criticised as mercenary, he may be seen as a dreamer, who requires a wife of beauty, wealth and status to match his vision of his own nobility.

Idealising himself denies him self-knowledge; idealising Hero masks fear and hatred of women. The altar scene is anticipated when Don John's false report convinces him that Don Pedro has betrayed him. Rather than blame his male friend, he has recourse to misogyny and its superstitions – 'for beauty is a witch, / Against whose charms faith melteth into blood' (II.1.135–6). That Don Pedro presents

QUESTION

'The forced marriages of Beatrice and Benedick and Hero and Claudio, both prompted by tricks, create an effect of emptiness and dissatisfaction.' How far would you agree with this view of *Much Ado About Nothing* and its effects?

Hero to Claudio already won says much about this fear, his emotional insecurity and his social ambition.

Claudio plays a minor role in the gulling of Benedick, a callow, overeager participant and a crude tease when his love-sickness becomes obvious. When Don John tells him Hero is 'disloyal', whereas Don Pedro 'will not think it', Claudio wonders, 'May this be so?' and vows, if it is, 'in the congregation, where I should wed, there will I shame her' (III.2.86–7 & 92). His aggressive denunciation, arising from a personal insecurity that causes him to make a fetish of honour, suggests that he has already tried and found her guilty before witnessing the evidence. The initial 'figure of a lamb' performing the 'feats of a lion' was heroic, larger than life, slightly incongruous. There is a similar excess to his punishment of Hero.

At the altar he dramatically seizes control of the marriage ceremony: 'Give not this rotten orange to your friend' (IV.1.27) becomes the more gratuitously arrogant and hurtful to Hero and Leonato when the source text is considered, with its mild complaint against the lady's dishonour. The sincerity of his indignation at her offence and his absolute belief in honour are unquestionable. 'She's but the sign and semblance of her honour' (line 28), he exclaims. He reiterates his astonishment at the gulf between her apparent modesty and actual corruption and his former ideal and present deluded belief in her degradation. In **similes** reminiscent of his own depiction as a lion in ferocity wearing a lamb's garment of softness and youth, he contrasts his former impression of her as 'Diana in her orb, / As chaste as is the bud ere it be blown' to his latter as 'Venus, or those pampered animals, / That rage in savage sensuality' (IV.1.50–1 & 54–5). The irrationality of his accusation is reinforced by its source – the bastard Don John, who has rebelled against his brother and is the product of unchastity. The contrasting images of Diana and Venus confirm that he cannot reconcile himself to Hero's sexuality or mortal imperfection. When he exclaims melodramatically, 'Oh Hero! What a Hero hadst thou been' (IV.1. 93), the punning with her name **ironically** underlines his distance from her reality and how undeserving of the stance of damning moral superiority he is. He concludes with **oxymorons** expressive

CONTEXT

Pamela Mason,1992, explains Claudio's malicious action through the military ethic: 'not simply a matter of Claudio having been deceived – for the honour of the regiment is at stake', p. 129.

of the pain of his disillusionment and the underlying love which his word play is intended to suppress: 'most foul, most fair, farewell / Thou pure impiety, and impious purity' (IV.1. 96–7). There is also irony, since the foulness and impiety are his illusions, and she has remained as she outwardly seems.

Beatrice pinpoints the flimsiness and base cruelty of Claudio's accusation. We applaud Benedick for undertaking to avenge the slight and our mean opinion of Claudio is confirmed when, after Hero has been reported dead, he can joke, 'We had like to have had our two noses snapped off with two old men without teeth' (V.1.112–13) and try to draw Benedick into banter to relieve his boredom. Benedick's insult to Claudio's courage, 'you break jests, as braggarts do their blades' (V.1.168–9), sticks.

Claudio's redemption is possible only if his youth and sincere repentance are emphasised. 'I have drunk poison' (V.1.215) is his reaction to Borachio's confession. Hero's 'image doth appear / In the rare semblance that I loved it first' (V.1. 220–1), which could be interpreted as shallow and immature, since he is still harping upon her outward beauty and spotless reputation. Yet his apology to Leonato appears heart-felt, 'Yet sinned I not, / But in mistaking' (V.1. 241–2) and his willingness to accept any penance of Leonato's invention humble. He agrees to marry Hero's cousin with tears of gratitude, though having first learned that she has double Hero's dowry.

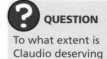

QUESTION

To what extent is Claudio deserving of Hero?

Claudio's public display of grief is intended to cancel out his earlier denunciation. He acknowledges his guilt in the epitaph and sues for forgiveness in the song. Don Pedro's announcement that 'the wolves have preyed' and his lyrical response to the first glimmering of light as the 'gentle day' that 'dapples the drowsy east with spots of grey' (V.3.25–7) symbolically acknowledges collective responsibility and heralds a new order cleansing a humbler Claudio of guilt. Yet he approaches the ceremony with tasteless bumptiousness, 'I'll hold my mind were she an Ethiop' (V.4.38), which taints the humility of 'I am your husband if you like of me' (V.1. 59). His amazement and gratitude at the miracle of Hero's restoration seem genuine, 'Another Hero?' (V.1. 62). He accepts that the constancy of the object of his love, tarnished only by his slander, is reborn with its death. Yet before the ceremony he teased Benedick about becoming a cuckold and afterwards he boasts about his prowess with his fists. His capacity for moral growth thus appears limited, whether by youth, social privilege, egotism or an unshakeable faith in male privilege and female subordination.

HERO

Hero's reticence is a sign both of innocence and of the superior market value of her relative youth, beauty, wealth and social position. Claudio's denunciation of her as 'but the sign and semblance of her honour' (IV.1.28) is **ironic**, since to play the marriageable virgin, she had not assumed a character and had only been a sign. Amongst female company, she displays a keen and flexible wit. Her strategy of praising Benedick and condemning Beatrice's pride has the desired effect. Urging Margaret to extol Benedick 'more than ever man did merit' (III.1.19) is a suave deflation, arising from knowledge of male vanity. Her directions to Margaret, 'steal into the pleachèd bower' (III.1.7) bespeaks her delicacy. A shrewd assessment of court intrigue is implicit in her **metaphors**: 'honeysuckles ripened by the sun, / Forbid the sun to enter: like favourites, / Made proud by princes' (lines 8–10). Her insight into the machinations of the ambitious, her ironically prophetic comments on love 'That only wounds by hearsay' (III.1.22), 'Some Cupid kills with arrows, some with traps' (III.1.106), and her boasts of Claudio's superiority to all other men, broaden her conventional character and make her dishonour more poignant.

Immediately before the wedding, Hero's innocence is emphasised in dialogue with Margaret: 'my heart is exceeding heavy' (III.4.19), she complains, at the prospect of losing her virginity, and is teased coarsely for it. Hero fusses over her dress to take her mind off her anxiety; she is conventional, not at all deep, but ladylike and deserving of sympathy.

Shy and deferential, she is defenceless against Claudio's denunciation. Humanised through the worries and wit she discloses to her lady friends, she embodies the enormous pressure upon the

CHECK THE BOOK

For a discussion of Hero's silence and her theatricality, see Roger Sales, 1987, pp. 82–9.

women of Messina to conform to a male ideal. She retains her dignity until she faints, protesting her innocence righteously: 'Is it not Hero? Who can blot that name with any just reproach?' (IV.1.74–5). Her character is further elevated by the Friar's insistence upon her innocence and Beatrice's spirited defence, as well as by her inability to comprehend the villainy which has been her undoing.

Her willingness to marry Claudio after he has disgraced her is problematic. She will enjoy the moral high ground in the marriage, since she has forgiven him and recovered her reputation; 'One Hero died defiled, but I do live, / And surely as I live, I am a maid' (V.4.63–4). Her fidelity to an unworthy man and her self-vindication in terms of a male code of honour have disappointed modern feminist critics. Yet she is true to herself as a conventional, romantic heroine, exemplary in her patience and forgiveness.

MINOR CHARACTERS

Ursula and Margaret

Ursula's is a minor, comic role. She teases Antonio about his age at the masked ball and she helps Hero to gull Beatrice She is vivacious, witty and mischievous. Margaret's is more significant: her affair with Borachio is exploited to disgrace Hero. Although she is not among the wedding guests, she would have heard of Hero's disgrace and yet she banters blithely with Benedick afterwards and does nothing to exonerate Hero. Borachio insists upon her ignorance of the plot and calls her 'just and virtuous' (V.1.269), which is questionable. Although Leonato blames her, she is included in the final wedding party. The ambiguity opens her character to interpretation.

Borachio boasts that he can make Margaret look out of her mistress's chamber window at any time of the night. The next morning her coarse, bawdy teasing of Hero does not imply chastity. She voices her envy of the rich in a garrulous, vulgar style. Yet she speaks impressively for the democracy of sexuality, 'Is there any harm in the heavier for a husband' (III.4.26), against the cant of honourably prim virginity. She outduels the love-sick Beatrice in

CHECK THE BOOK

Cedric Watts, 'Woman and Convention', considers Margaret and her unsatisfactory character, 'lively, sprightly and confident' before and after the disaster, see Cookson and Loughrey, 1989, p. 113.

Minor characters continued

CHECK THE BOOK

Pamela Mason, 1992, shows how drama was created in the 1988 Renaissance production by making Margaret a worldly wise character whose reputation was in danger.

wit, with subtly barbed quips, as saucily provocative, though more obscene, with the blatant innuendo of, 'To have a man come over me' and 'Give us the swords, we have bucklers of our own' (V.2.6 & 13).

By evening up the cast of male and female characters, Ursula and Margaret make the battle of the sexes seem fair and enhance the overall impression of female wit and gaiety. Margaret's relationship with Borachio underlines the corruption and corrupting influence of the aristocracy, whom she, like Borachio, serves. She exposes the folly of romantic idealisation which culminates in Hero's disgrace and the emptiness of a code of honour which preserves male preeminence and subjugates women. Some productions have emphasised her jealousy, bitterness and ambition. Her resemblance to Beatrice strengthens the case for earthy realism in sexual relations.

Don Pedro

Of Messina's aristocrats, Don Pedro, prince of Arragon, ranks highest. Although the social gap between him and Leonato is smaller than in the sources, everyone defers to him. He has 'bestowed much honour' (I.1.7) upon Claudio and as his patron woos Hero in his guise. When informed of Hero's alleged infidelity, Don Pedro sanctions Claudio's vengeance by offering to 'join with thee to disgrace her' (III.2.94). Such is Don Pedro's influence and arrogance that Claudio offers to accompany him on his departure from Messina on the wedding day.

CHECK THE BOOK

Roger Sales,1987, portrays Don Pedro as an arrogant Spaniard – 'this camp, middle-aged bachelor will return to Arragon to find another clutch of impressionable, young men', p. 68.

He is always grand and never subordinate. He has a Renaissance prince's belief in the prerogative of his power: ''tis once, thou lovest, / And I will fit thee with a remedy' (I.1.244–5), absolutely confident that he will win Hero for Claudio. He looks upon courtship as a battle to be won with military guile and force, 'take her hearing prisoner with the force / … of my amorous tale' (I.1.250–1). When he flirtatiously offers himself to Beatrice, she demurs, as he expects – 'your grace is too costly for wear every day' (II.1.250). He shows princely magnanimity when she blushes at a *faux pas*: 'Your silence most offends me, and to be merry, best becomes you' (lines 252–3). Perceiving that Benedick and Beatrice are well suited, he successfully conspires to bring them together. He has a sense of fun, deceiving Benedick with relish and teasing him with gentle and playful energy afterwards. He displays his wit when he parodies Dogberry without malice: 'First I ask thee what they have done, thirdly I ask thee what's their offence, sixthly …' (V.1.195–6).

Hearing the truth about Don John's plot, he is conscience-stricken and contrite. He joins with Claudio to perform the rites of atonement at Hero's tomb and speaks the verse which propels the play towards joyful reconciliation: 'The wolves have preyed, and look, the gentle day / Before the wheels of Phoebus round about / Dapples the drowsy east with spots of grey' (V.3.25–8). There is harmony in his soul, as he had earlier savoured Balthasar's song and later calls for music at the wedding. There is both humility and pomp in his wonderful image of Phoebus dropping light in the east to herald the advent of another day. The image of the preying wolves can be seen as a debonair acknowledgement of his own destructive error and the need now to forgive and forget and carry on with life.

Yet Don Pedro has not appealed to modern taste. He is the benefactor denied the marital joys he prepares for others, whether owing to pride or age or different sexual leanings. He exerts himself to arrange the affairs of others and maintain a position of superiority himself. His willingness to join Claudio in slandering Hero seems cowardly. He is arrogant and weak when he echoes Don John: 'I stand dishonoured … To link my dear friend to a common stale' (IV.1.58–9). 'On my honour' (V.1.123) is the phrase he uses to introduce his outline of the evidence against Hero. His concept of honour and of his own importance are blinding. He is callous and peremptory in his treatment of Antonio and Leonato after Hero's reported death. His reaction to the news of Hero's innocence, 'Runs not this speech like iron through your blood?' (V.1.214), could be construed as shifting the responsibility on to Claudio and absolving himself, although the contrary is equally justified – that he is sensitive to how much worse Claudio, who loved and denounced Hero, must be feeling. Nevertheless, he does not dwell on his guilt but heaps the blame on Don John, 'composed and framed of treachery' (V.1.218). He is a Mediterranean aristocrat for whom gesture, show and allegiance to a code of honour are paramount.

> **CONTEXT**
>
> Prejudice against the illegitimate, common in the Elizabethan age, is also to be found in *King Lear*, where the villain, like Don John, is an unbeliever and epicurean – a believer in pleasure as the greatest good.

CONTEXT

Under Henry VIII
(who reigned from
1509 to 1547), the
father of Elizabeth
I, England broke
with the Church of
Rome and
established an
independent
Church of England
which, during the
last years of Henry
and the reign of
Edward VII,
became
increasingly
Protestant in its
theology and
practices.

Leonato and Antonio

Leonato, governor of Messina, appears as a tender, overprotective father, gracious host, affectionate brother and kindly uncle. He acknowledges his 'grey hairs and bruise of many days' (V.1.65), regrets that he is too old to become a father again and in Antonio has a brother with senescent palsy and dry palm. Claudio dismisses them as 'two old men without teeth' (V.1.112–13). Leonato's deliberate, sententious style typifies the man in decline. His exchanges with the messenger in the opening scene express general truths with complacent sentimentality: 'A kind overflow of kindness … How much better is it to weep at joy, than to joy at weeping' (I.1.20–22). The **aphoristic** style, with its complex parallels, balance and **antithesis**, bespeaks the detachment of one reflecting superficially upon a life in which he is no longer passionately involved. His welcome to Don Pedro is so convoluted that the feeling and meaning can be lost: 'Never came trouble to my house in the likeness of your grace: for trouble being gone, comfort should remain: but when you depart from me, sorrow abides, and happiness takes his leave' (I.1.73–5). This is not the brisk language of a busy governor; these are the laboured **metaphors** of an overdeferential, scheming aristocrat. He is constantly polite, always distinguishing the person he addresses with a title, even his daughter and niece. Often interrupted or gently teased, whether owing to elderly tolerance or slowness on the uptake, he never takes offence. Tragicomic complications arise when the Watch with their even slower wits try and fail to inform him of the plot against Hero. 'Neighbours, you are tedious' (III.5.14), he complains, urging them with polite familiarity to hurry up. Dogberry's offer to 'bestow' all his tediousness on Leonato is comic, since Leonato is tedious and so obtuse that he fails to see what Dogberry is driving at. Yet his response, 'All thy tediousness on me, eh?' (III.5.18) is gentle and good-humoured.

Age and social insecurity make Leonato preoccupied with status: he wants Hero and Beatrice to marry advantageously. He is underhand: Antonio evidently spies for him and the ball is masked; he delights in gulling Benedick under Don Pedro's direction. He is patriarchal, warning Beatrice that her wit may deny her a husband and telling Hero how to behave when wooed.

The denunciation scene exposes Leonato's friendship with Don Pedro as a sham. The distrust and aggression Leonato's courtesy masks is also brought into the open. His efforts to hurry the ceremony up and to retain control which Claudio gradually wrests from him indicate his dominance of Hero whose marriage was to be the crowning event of his social life. His failure to understand the accusations immediately is a presumption of Hero's innocence. Yet once they have sunk in, he is credulous and dwells upon his dishonour rather than her suffering: 'hath no man's dagger here a point for me?' (IV.1.102). When she faints, he rashly gives voice to a wish that she should die or he would finish her off himself, not to spare her a lifetime of dishonour but to revenge her sin. In the prolonged lamentations and the later threats of vengeance that follow, the proliferation of the first person 'I' or 'mine' reveals a callous and possessive egocentricity, assumption of male privilege and superiority and a latent aggression underlying his courtly, senile mask. He embodies the irrationality and impotent violence which are the hidden face of the Italian courtier, patriarch and old man. His egotism appears more culpable on the page than in the theatre, where it deepens our sympathy for Hero.

When (V.1) Antonio begins by attempting to appease Leonato's anger and then has himself to be restrained from attacking Claudio, the result is usually farce. Nevertheless, it heightens the seriousness of the slander and the callousness of the accusers while belabouring Leonato's point, 'there was never yet philosopher, / That could endure the tooth-ache patiently' (V.1.35–6). He has adduced such a collection of clichés and aphorisms that he appears more ridiculous and vain than pitiable. He has had his certainties about life overturned and his habitual character shattered, ultimately to his own redemption. He now reproves Claudio with, 'Thou hast wronged mine innocent child and me' (V.1.63), for the first time putting Hero's dishonour before his own. His indignation when Borachio confesses is warm and righteous, his forgiveness of Claudio and Don Pedro magnanimous and the penance he imposes just and curative. It might be argued that he reverts to type in making Hero marry the man who had disgraced her. Unable to transcend the conventions of his culture and his class, he is delighted to see Hero's dishonour wiped away through marriage. However,

QUESTION

Do the darker overtones of distrust and tyranny undermine the comedy of old age?

she does not demur and forgiveness and acceptance of guilt are endorsed in the final scene of reconciliation.

Antonio is a comic figure whose function is to contribute to the family atmosphere and add to the picture of old age. He acts as Leonato's agent, misreporting to him Don Pedro's plans for Hero's wooing. He raises a laugh at the masked ball for his inability to conceal dry, elderly hand and palsied head. When he counsels his brother against excessive grief as unmanly and destructive, he appears kindly, and when he too is so provoked by Claudio's arrogance that he tries to start a fight with him, he cuts a ridiculous yet sympathetic figure.

The picture of old age in the play as a whole is unflattering – conventional, hypocritical, rash and morally blind. The old are responsible for the world which youth has to strive against and try to remake.

> **CONTEXT**
>
> *King Lear* is Shakespeare's most savage portrayal of irrational anger and possessiveness in the elderly.

Don John

Don John is merely sketched as a melodramatic villain, a stereotypical bastard serving a thematic and narrative function. His awkwardly repetitive opening line, 'I thank you, I am not of many words, but I thank you' (I.1.116), in response to gracious words of welcome and reconciliation, is ludicrously overblown and vacuous. To Conrade he complains, 'I am trusted with a muzzle, and enfranchised with a clog' (I.3.24), a resentful outsider who cannot abide constraints – 'There is no measure in the occasion that breeds, therefore the sadness is without limit' (I.3.3–4) – even though the isolation his egotism demands adds to his misery. His overuse of the first person singular indicates his egocentricity. He insists that malice is honesty or truth to the base selfishness within everyone: 'I cannot hide what I am' (I.3.10); 'I am a plain dealing villain' (I.3.23–4); 'let me be that I am, and seek not to alter me' (I.3.27).

In celebrating his honest villainy, he is cynical: virtue is always a façade. He rails against Claudio's promotion, 'that young start-up' (I.3.48), at his expense, which supplies him with a motive. Although he causes Claudio distress at the masked ball by hinting that Don Pedro has taken Hero for himself, Borachio is architect of the scheme to disgrace her. Don John's lack of ingenuity and initiative makes him baser and less admirable.

His language is stiff and overelaborate. His use of balance, **antithesis** and **alliteration** would be courtly like Leonato's, except that his constant subject is himself: 'I must be sad when I have cause, and smile at no man's jests: eat when I have stomach ... laugh when I am merry, and claw no man in his humour' (I.3.10–13). Whereas the logical structure implies intelligence and control, it is too rigid for wit and too egocentric and mean in its imagery to be aphoristic. Though cowardly, underhand and ineffectual, he has a shrewd understanding of the court. When he does make insinuations about Hero, he plays upon tensions in the court about honour and status which make friendships fragile.

Don John's malevolent deception is balanced by those benign deceptions which draw Beatrice and Benedick together. Borachio, with the insight of the jealous and thwarted inferior, while carrying on a cynical affair with Margaret, knows how to exploit the aristocrats' nervous, blinding exaltation of honour and virginity. Don John also has the measure of his brother and his protégé, adopting the understated 'disloyal' to imply reluctance to sully his honour with exact representation of her crime and, cutting himself off with, 'I will disparage her no farther' (III.2.95), as though conscious of former faults.

Only in the denunciation scene does Don John show his hand in public. He backs up the charges and with assumed righteous indignation disarms Hero by first exaggerating her crimes and then pretending that he is sorry for her: 'There is not chastity enough in language, / Without offence to utter them: thus, pretty lady, / I am sorry for thy much misgovernment' (IV.1.90–2). Once she has fainted, he sweeps her other accusers out of the room before she has the chance to recover and respond. Only here, does he show initiative and resource.

Beatrice instinctively recoils from Don John, who locks 'tartly' and causes her heartburn and Benedick has the prescience to suspect him at once, 'Whose spirits toil in frame of villainies' (IV.1.182). Defying

CHECK THE BOOK
Richard Levin, 'Crime and Cover-up', Harold Bloom, ed., 1988, argues that Don John is not just a figure of melodrama; he represents the 'evil within society', p. 79.

**CHECK
THE BOOK**
J. Mulryne, 1965,
shows how the
darker themes of
the play infuse
structure and
characterisation.

the codes of their society, they can see him as he is. Cowardly, he runs away the moment suspicion looks in his direction. That he is brought back at the end of the play symbolises the intrinsic flaw in Messina's code of honour.

Borachio and Conrade

Borachio, like his counterpart, Margaret, is immediately distinguished by energy and resource: 'as I was smoking a musty room, comes me the prince and Claudio, hand in hand, in conference: I whipped me behind the arras' (I.3.42–4). In Messina spying for personal advancement is not egregious. His plot to disgrace Hero is clever and his exploitation of Margaret's sexual frailty base. Drunkenness (*borraccia* is Italian for hipflask) after taking his reward plunges him more deeply into sin for which he already feels some remorse while references to 'the devil my master' (III.1.126–7) blame Don John for corrupting him with money.

Borachio raves about 'what a deformed thief this fashion is' (III.3.107), amazed at how easy it was to exploit Margaret and deceive Claudio. Conrade replies that Borachio must be giddy with the fashion too so to digress and just before the curtain Benedick, apologising for his change of heart, remarks that 'man is a giddy thing' (V.4.104). The eavesdropping Watch misconstrue Borachio as referring to an actual thief 'who borrows money in God's name … and never paid, that now men grow hard-hearted and will lend nothing for God's sake' (V.1. 275–7). The obvious **satiric** point is that appearances deceive and are easily contrived by the unscrupulous. Another is that life is constantly changing and that fixed standards of honour invite self-deception. Borachio remarks that Claudio and Don Pedro were 'planted, placed, and possessed' (III.3.122) as they mistook Margaret for Hero, contradicting the laws of nature and time in their insistence upon honour. Confession redeems Borachio and contributes to the final reconciliation; responsibility remains with Don John.

Conrade is a passive, extraneous character introduced for the sake of symmetry, comedy and satire. He insists upon his social and intellectual superiority to the Watch as a gentleman and scholar. A true gentleman would not dishonour an innocent virgin or belittle those less privileged than himself.

The Watch

The Watch appear once Don John has sprung his plot. They provide instant and constant comic relief during the most painful passage of the play. With the addition of these humbler characters, a fuller and more convincing portrait of a complete society is painted. The principal comedy among the aristocracy comprises verbal wit and deception. Dogberry's incompetence adds sentimental farce. His attempt to impose his authority upon the Watch parodies the futile patriarchy of Messina.

Dogberry's fondness for complex language he does not understand is an aspect of his vanity. When he and Verges try and fail to tell Leonato about Don John's plot, he is prevented from coming to the point by his open and covert boasts about his superiority to Verges in youth, intellect and size. It is the fact that, as Conrade puts it, Dogberry is an ass, that makes his boastful self-confidence so funny. Whenever he tries to show off his knowledge or authority, he gets the word wrong, which creates some accidental satire and comedy. The comedy of the Watch is verbal, like Beatrice's and Benedick's, except that we laugh at their linguistic incompetence, not their verbal dexterity. His guidelines for the Watch – inaction, for which the Elizabethan Watch was notorious – are a comic *tour de force*.

Dogberry's obsequious assertions of superiority to Verges when he calls upon Leonato are comically transparent and ineffectual. When Leonato becomes impatient with the tedious account, Dogberry's reply, 'if I were as tedious as a king, I could find in my heart to bestow it all of your worship' (III.5.116–17) is funny in various ways: he has misunderstood another long word; he unwittingly undermines himself while trying to curry favour by revealing a latent ambition and disdain for Leonato.

Dogberry's outburst of indignation when Conrade calls him an ass is comic both because he is an ass and because he is unaware of it. His repeating a rhetorical request that he could be written down an ass is comic because he has been written down an ass in the text of

CHECK THE BOOK
For a discussion of the Watch as an expression of 'official bumbledom' see John Russell Brown, 1979, pp. 73–7.

QUESTION

What does the
Watch contribute
to the play
without which it
would be weaker?

the play and it is imprinted on the imagination of the audience. The
comedy of his self-defence as a 'wise fellow', an 'officer', 'a
householder' and 'as pretty a piece of flesh as any is in Messina'
(IV.2.65–7) is sentimental rather than savage. It is not that Dogberry
is none of these things, merely that none of them will ever make him
wise. The comedy becomes broader when he adds to the catalogue
of his attainments with a disordered and increasingly trivial list. He
helps to universalise the problem of self-deception inherent in the
main plots.

His description of the thief Deformed is a ridiculous manifestation
of vulgar superstition and scapegoating. His Deformed is no more
or less real than Claudio's disgraceful Hero: blaming others for
private sins is universal.

The Friar

Although the Friar is less character than plot-mechanism, he, like
the other characters, notes and deceives. Observation of Hero
convinces him of her innocence and he so questions her that she can
show it. He correctly deduces misprision as the source of her
dishonour and prescribes another benevolent deception, which
works, although too little time has elapsed for Claudio to be
transformed.

As a priest, he also has a unique spiritual perspective. He knows
how the human spirit operates, which he expresses in long speeches
in **blank verse** and in aphorism. He is the voice of reason,
moderation and wisdom with an active faith in the holiness of life
and the benevolence of providence. 'Let wonder seem familiar'
(V.4.70), he proclaims before the curtain falls, urging the cast and
audience to consider the unexpected good fortune of Hero's rebirth
and her marriage to Claudio and Beatrice's to Benedick. The final
reconciliation of man with nature is strengthened through him.

THEMES

NOTHINGNESS

The throw-away, take-it-or-leave-it titles of romantic comedies like *Much Ado About Nothing* draw attention to their unseriousness and openness to interpretation. Emphasis falls upon the subjectivity of love and the life-and-death struggle which it engenders, ending in marriage. Comedy, the titles imply, is therapeutic recreation from the serious yet narrowing business of life, which promotes reconciliation with nature and oneself. Though the lovers' unions after their testing ordeals be inevitable, the titles also suggest that they are fragile and mysterious.

The major ado or complication of *Much Ado* springs from Claudio's denunciation of Hero on the basis of a trick, a misconception, a nothing. The minor ado is the deception which unites Beatrice and Benedick at the point that Hero and Claudio separate. Claudio had yearned to possess the 'jewel' (I.l.134) of her beauty, wealth and honour or virginity. Humbled by his error in rejecting her, he is grateful for her generous, charitable forgiveness. In spite of the happy endings, love remains a mysterious product of illusion. Balthasar's song, 'Sigh no more, ladies' (II.3.53) emphasises the irrationality of the unending male quest for love. Its origin is sexual, since 'the world', as Benedick puts it, 'must be peopled' (II.3.197), and social, 'Taming', as Beatrice puts it, 'my wild heart to thy loving hand' (III.1.112) and saying to proud and solitary 'Contempt, farewell, and maiden pride, adieu' (III.1.109). It arises from nothing tangible but like the poet's imagination or the will of God it perpetuates life and affronts ultimate extinction and meaninglessness.

'Nothing' was an Elizabethan **euphemism** for female genitalia. Shakespeare pokes fun at the fuss created by male desire to gain control of the female nothing. Characters pun bawdily on 'nothing' whenever the opportunity arises as well as on 'will', which stood both for desire and the actual penis. It reminds us of the animal basis of love, which Claudio had excised. Psychoanalytic criticism sees romantic idealisation as a defence against the fear of female

> **CONTEXT**
>
> The subjectivity of perception, illusion and the blindness of love are common themes of Shakespeare's comedy, as the titles suggest – *As You Like It, All's Well that Ends Well, A Midsummer's Night's Dream*.

sexuality and death. Hero does not speak, a sexual icon upon which Claudio projects an ideal of honour to mask her sexuality. He is the first hero mentioned, 'doing in the figure of a lamb the feats of a lion' (I.1.12). He had proven the strength of his will on the battlefield; in peace his arena is the drawing room. Elizabethan audiences were accustomed to Hero as a female name from the devoted lover of Greek legend, revived in Marlowe's *Hero and Leander*. It reverberates from Don John's contemptuous, 'Leonato's Hero, your Hero, every man's Hero' (III.3.78) to Claudio's disillusioned, 'Oh Hero! What a Hero hadst thou been' (IV.1.93). **Ironically** his vision of her virtue was clouded by deception when he ceased trusting the 'counsel of his heart' (IV.1.95). It reechoes again at her unveiling: from Claudio, 'Another Hero!', from the bride herself, 'One Hero died defiled, but I do live' and from Don Pedro, 'the former Hero! The Hero that is dead' (V.4.62–5). By playing upon the name as a male ideal of extraordinary virtue and strength, Shakespeare invites us to see Claudio's Hero as a narcissistic projection of his own self-ideal. He appears as an elaborate 'figure' or verbal construction or **metaphor**; so Hero is an artifice doomed to shatter at its first contact with reality. As a projection of male honour created to escape from mortality, Hero had to die for her sake and Claudio's. Losing his illusion, he gains her reality. The connotations are conservative: Hero stands by her man and is a maid at the altar. Nevertheless, the relationship becomes rooted in the reality of patient and generous love.

CHECK THE BOOK

Karen Newman, in 'Mistaking in *Much Ado*', Harold Bloom, ed., 1988, investigates 'credulity and self-deception' in the play, pp. 123–32.

NOTING

Ever since a Victorian pointed out that the Elizabethans pronounced nothing as noting, the central importance of noting, spying and eavesdropping has been remarked. After all, if Claudio and Don Pedro had not spied on what they mistook as Hero, the wedding would have gone forward, and if Beatrice and Benedick had not eavesdropped, they would have remained scornful celibates. Claudio asks Benedick, 'didst thou note the daughter of Signor Leonato?' to which he replies, 'I noted her not, but I looked on her' (I.1.19–20), already pointing to the subjectivity of perception. If beauty is an illusion, the lover's feelings will change however constant the object of his adoration.

Both songs, 'Sigh no more' (II.3.53) sung in the orchard before the gulling of Benedick, and the epitaph and song at Hero's tomb are apologies for male inconstancy. 'Sigh no more' paves the way for the changes in Benedick and Claudio, the one into and the other from a lover, and acts as a commentary on male behaviour. It implies that male inconstancy, or fundamental ambivalence, with 'One foot in sea, and one on shore' (II.3.55), is inveterate and irrational. It contrasts the relatively stable and the utterly fluid, dream and reality. Marriage to Hero will earth Claudio, but his dream or illusion attracted him to her. Noting is precise and self-conscious; male intellectuality makes emotions insecure and relationships problematic.

Hero is wooed from behind a mask as Claudio watches, noted by Benedick and Don John who are also noting Don Pedro, while the audience notes them all. A few carefully aimed words mislead Claudio into mistaking what he notes and seeing the infidelity of his fears. The spying of Antonio and Borachio produces minor and major complications. In the gulling of Beatrice and Benedick the tricksters and the tricked are noting one another under the observant eyes of the audience. Moreover, false impressions are created so that each of the overhearing scenes becomes a play within the play which drives each eavesdropper to love his former antagonist. There follow comic scenes in which Beatrice and Benedick are noted as they yield to the compulsion to play the part of the melancholy lover and to try to cover it up with physical sickness (III.2 & III.4). Both wedding scenes and the performance at Hero's tomb can be considered plays within the play. In each, **dramatic irony** is prominent in the discrepant awareness among the characters and between stage and audience. This predisposition to note and misread makes the comedy more sophisticated by foregrounding illusion and comments on the society of Messina. Among the aristocracy, manners are refined, hospitality generous and the play of illusion, as the masked ball indicates, compulsive. Its morality is rigid and its ceremonies and entertainments static and cold. In such a highly conventionalised society with its constant round of social observances and sophisticated play of wit and illusion, insecurity, deception and self-deception are rampant and real emotions and thoughts remain hidden and suppressed.

CHECK THE BOOK

For a discussion of noting, see the Introduction to the Arden Edition of *Much Ado* and Cookson and Loughrey, 1989, and for mistaking see Harold Bloom, ed., 1988, pp. 123–4.

Insecurity is implicit in the rashness with which Hero is condemned even by her own father; Beatrice and Benedick discover their mutual love by separating themselves from the court. When Benedick commits himself to Beatrice, he breaks through illusion and begins to discover himself.

The Watch parody the ruling class. Ironically their distorted vision uncovers the truth to which their betters remain obstinately blind. Through misunderstanding they conjure up a fantastic thief named Deformed, which comments on the gross distortion of the truth in the image of Hero in Don John's slander and Claudio's idealisation.

The play ends with music, dancing and marriage which Benedick wholeheartedly celebrates, man being a changeable creature. All masks are removed for the festivities; he no longer hides behind a profession but is openly stating what he has found himself to be. Noting is suspended, but as Don John is to be brought back to justice, such moments of frankness and gaiety in the court can only be temporary.

QUESTION

Does the play suggest that in marriage the characters will be able to relax and remove their constricting social masks?

ILLUSION AND REALITY

The centrality of illusion and reality is established with the false accusation against Hero. Beatrice called Claudio 'civil as an orange' and 'jealous' (II.1.2.23) overemphasis upon male honour and female virginity in a patriarchal society fosters illusion. 'Give not this rotten orange to your friend' (IV.1.24) Claudio storms. His **metaphor** means hypocrisy – wholesome in appearance but morally corrupt within. Claudio denounces Hero for the supposed discrepancy between her 'outward graces' (IV.1.94) as chaste as Diana - ironically true – and her unruly blood or corrupt heart – ironically an illusion. The power of illusion is enhanced when fabrications oblige Beatrice and Benedick to express their real feelings of love for each other.

Claudio's idealised love for Hero masked fear and aggression, which erupts in the chapel. Beatrice's and Benedick's love began in illusory antagonism and was sealed in aggression with the demand for Claudio's death. Claudio's wrong had to be righted, his character redeemed and Hero had to get her heart's desire. **Blank verse** and references to death and rebirth elevate the marriage ceremony. Emphasis is upon the constancy of her affection. Claudio's misapprehension and slander buried her worth. Now that his vision has cleared, her reality can be revealed.

The constant play of illusion raises the issue of the subjectivity of perception and makes drama itself a theme. With plays within plays, the audience becomes aware of the actors playing characters, who are themselves playing other parts within the play. Although illusion entertains and can lead to the revelation of truth, it is also potentially destructive, as with Hero. The question is raised of what is real. Appropriately for a comedy, the answer would appear to be love, even though it too originates in illusion.

LOVE

Much Ado explores the nature of true love, though less romantically than comedies in which disguise, illusion and misunderstanding invest love with a power of ineffable mystery. It is realistic and critical. Its romantic lovers are flawed and lack charm, its cynics compelling and charismatic.

The first scene introduces the theme of love. Vacationing soldiers are to invade the peaceful court of Messina. Claudio, recent war hero, proclaims his love for that 'jewel' (I.1.27) Hero whom his patron, Don Pedro, offers to woo in disguise. Benedick scoffs, pointing out the discrepancy between Claudio's illusions and Hero's reality. A woman curbs a soldier's necessary freedom and thirst for adventure then cuckolds him for his pains. Claudio links the romantic and martial, his 'war-thoughts' (I.1.227) having given way in peace to 'thronging soft and delicate desires' (I.1.229) for Hero as a wife. He seeks self-transcendence, to which Hero is a means. So she remains silent, an object of male projection and idealisation. Claudio's aggression is not diverted. Don Pedro's proposal to 'take her hearing prisoner with the force / And strong encounter of my amorous tale' (I.1.250–1) implies that aggression must be contained within sexual love, not refined from it.

Beatrice and Benedick put forward a deflating, antagonistic image of sexual relations. 'You are a rare parrot teacher', Benedick insults

CHECK THE BOOK

P. and M. Mueschke, 'Much Ado About Nothing', John Russell Brown, ed., 1979, argue that 'the theme of this comedy is honour, that its spirit is less joyous than reflective and that courtship . . .is presented as an imminent threat to masculine honour', p. 130.

CHECK THE FILM

In Branagh's film of *Much Ado,* there are panoramas of the clear blue skies and soft hills of Tuscany and women bathing and dressing in white, which associate love with the feminine and natural.

Love continued

with one animal image and Beatrice replies with 'A bird of my tongue is better than a beast of yours' (I.1.103–4). **Ironically,** Claudio soon complains that his 'treasure's' beauty has bewitched his patron, so insecure and deluded has his idealisation made him.

Beatrice objects to privileged male pretensions: 'would it not grieve a woman to be overmastered with a piece of valiant dust' (II.1.43–4); **bathos** and **oxymoron** express her revulsion from conventional female subjugation. Her **metaphor** for 'wooing, wedding and repenting… as a Scotch jig, a measure and a cinquepace' (II.1.52–4) ironically foreshadows the pattern the relationship of Claudio and Hero traces. With constant allusions to birth, death and the brevity of life, to heaven and hell, pretensions and folly and promise and disappointment, Beatrice armours herself against rejection. Attracting attention with witty disdain, she hides the pain of her anomalous position as poorer, older spinster cousin. Apparent indifference to marriage frees her to attack the vanity and hypocrisy of male privilege and honour.

Benedick's reputation as exploiter of male privilege is confirmed by Leonato and Beatrice, who complains that he wears 'his faith but as the fashion of his hat' (I.1.55–6). He expects of women a fidelity he has not himself practised, but knows that the code of honour which regulates the conduct of war is inadequate to control sexual aggression in times of peace. His preferred animal image is the bull, with its cuckold horns, but other animals abound: 'pluck off the bull's horns' (I.1.196); 'hang me in a bottle like a cat and shoot at me' (I.1.191); 'here is good horse to hire' (I.1.197–8). These images communicate aggression and fear of self-mutilation or castration. He craves male bonding as protection from women but is too spontaneous and sensual to trust an abstract code. He gloats when he believes that Don Pedro has stolen Hero, since it confirms his belief in the impossibility of sexual fidelity.

The characters are so paired and grouped to represent each other's hidden or darker side. The play opens after Don Pedro has crushed the rebellion of his illegitimate brother, a hint that Don John enacts his brother's latent aggression. He unquestioningly believes in Don John's picture of Hero's hypocrisy and hidden immorality. Don

John's 'I cannot hide that I am' (I.3.10) represents the baser reality which keeps surfacing in the play.

Don Pedro's and Claudio's repressed violence explodes in their malicious defamation of Hero in a scene fraught with unsettling ironies. Claudio avenges the insult to his honour dishonourably. The ease of his deception hints at a secret wish to dishonour Hero or see her as a whore. 'Out on thy seeming!' he cries. He had thought her a Diana, 'As chaste as is the bud ere it is blown' (IV.1.51–2). Floral and classical imagery tell us less about Hero than Claudio's fantasy. The contrast between the images of Diana and Venus, with which he represents her supposed sensuality, recall his depiction as lion and lamb, one who aspires to an unattainable ideal. Claudio and Leonato exalt honour above humanity. Leonato actually begs that Hero should die rather than wake dishonoured. In a twenty-three-line speech, he uses 'I' twelve times: wounded vanity and idealisation of honour have compromised paternal love.

In the orchard before the eavesdropping, Benedick complacently reviews his immunity to women's tempting physical and moral charms. Afterwards he interrogates himself and decides to be 'horribly in love' (II.3.191). He accepts realistically his human imperfection and agrees to settle down. He kindly and humbly pities Beatrice for loving a man as unworthy as himself and honestly owns to sexual desire for her – 'the world must be peopled' (II.3.197).

To see the misogynist brought low by love, freshly shaven and perfumed in the latest fashion, is funny. More seriously love is seen as a universal, ameliorating force of change combating egotism and uniting two separate individuals as one. Through their love, Beatrice overcomes her fear of death and Benedick his fear of impotence.

Before they plight their troths, Beatrice has also been humbled. 'Benedick, love on', she urges, 'I will requite thee, / Taming my wild heart to thy loving hand' (III.1.110–111). Her willingness to subordinate herself after having so resented male privilege is touching. Her command, 'Kill Claudio!' (IV.1.279) as soon as Benedick avows his love, is rich in comic irony. Love has mitigated

CHECK THE BOOK

Donald Stauffer considers *Much Ado* Shakespeare's 'severest criticism to date of the weakness lying in romantic love', John Russell Brown, 1979, p. 87.

her disdain but it has not altered her character. Benedick concludes they are 'too wise to woo peaceably' (V.2.54) and stops her mouth with a kiss.

Mutual love detaches Beatrice and Benedick from Messina and connects them with what is more permanent. Beatrice exacts commitment to her, not abstract social ideals. She wants open, honest reciprocal love and sympathy. She redefines manliness in her tirade against Claudio: it is not heroic glory but the defence of truth and emotional honesty in daily life. The compromise she and Benedick reach not to woo peacefully but to retain some antagonism – to 'love no more than reason' (V.4.74) – guarantees balance and freshness through unceasing examination and constant redefinition. Theirs is the model of true love.

Claudio is incapable of love until his romantic idealisation has been shattered. Through the expressions of regret, the song and epitaph at Hero's tomb, the process of remorse is telescoped. Claudio learns that love is unchanging. Hero's soul is immune to change, slander or to death. Having learned the meaning of true love, he is fit to have Hero restored to him.

Benedick had complained of the boring restrictions of married life compelling caged man to 'sigh away Sundays' (I.1.149). His relationship with Beatrice is destined to last because there are no illusions to be shattered – they know each other so well – and because of the certainty that they will be able to keep each other entertained through the constant expression of their wit and their fidelity to their feelings.

JEALOUSY AND HONOUR

Claudio in his malleable and destructive jealousy might be a younger Othello, fearless and resourceful in battle, easily undone by love. Jealousy is implicit in the pictures Benedick creates of cuckolded husbands trapped at home by faithless wives. He instantly dislikes Hero and jealously resents Claudio for turning from soldier to lover. The openness and realism of his relationship with Beatrice rids it of jealousy.

QUESTION

How can love, based on illusion and deception, also be portrayed as necessary and realistic?

Leonato jealously protects Hero's honour. His initial horror and rage and his prolonged distress at the disgrace of the fruit of his old age and vessel of future hope proclaim the depth and strength of his attachment. Repetition, exaggeration and profuse imagery in uncontrolled tirades point to a mind pushed to the verge of insanity by despair. His love is possessive and authoritarian: she is his, he keeps repeating, and his honour depends upon her chastity. Although she suffers, empathy is suppressed in anxiety about his reputation and the frustration of his dream. When on slender evidence he adjudges her promiscuous, he expresses the wish that she had never been born. He suffers for the patriarchal belief in his right to determine and control her behaviour.

Claudio, a bashful lover, puts Hero on such a high pedestal that Don Pedro's offer to woo for him is a relief. 'Can the world buy such a jewel' (I.1.134) is conventional romantic hyperbole. His jealous tendency becomes apparent in his fear of being tied down: 'I would scarce trust myself … if Hero would be my wife' (I.1. 144–5). When Don Pedro sanctions his choice, he grows suspicious: 'You speak this to fetch me in' (I.1.165).

Claudio's jealous temperament is more sharply defined during the masked ball – he spies while Don Pedro woos. When Don John makes mischief and he believes that Don Pedro is wooing for himself, he becomes a misogynist: 'beauty is a witch' which can melt a friend's loyalty 'into blood' (II.1.135–6). Like Othello, he is proud and has to be alone to hide the marks of jealousy. Beatrice sees through Claudio, 'civil as an orange, and something of that jealous complexion' (II.1. 233–4). Speechless when Don Pedro presents Hero to him, Claudio remains constrained by jealous resentment.

Recently covered in glory, newly in love, of a jealous temperament, Claudio is easy prey to Don John. 'Her chamber window entered' (III.2.82) – an obvious vaginal symbol; 'every man's Hero' (III.2.78); 'a ruffian at her chamber window … vile encounters … a thousand times in secret' (IV.1.85–8) – nightmare images of cynical infidelity to an inexperienced youth who had believed in his betrothed's virginity. He obtains his ocular proof from 'afar off in the orchard' (III.3.123), does not consult Hero and puts his trust in

CONTEXT

Honour and jealousy have tragic consequences in *Hamlet* and *Othello*.

a bastard 'composed and framed of treachery' (V.1.218) whose revolt against his patron he was instrumental in suppressing. Implicitly, he trusts any man before the most spotless woman. He dwells upon her apparent hypocrisy when he denounces Hero. His jealousy is softened only by Hero's reported death. His willingness to marry a cousin unseen, 'were she an Ethiop' (V.4.88) signifies the death of possessive jealousy and the birth of forgiveness. In byplay before the final wedding, Claudio is no longer an observer standing aloof. He teases Benedick about being cuckolded: he is a 'double dealer' (V.4.109) who 'thinks upon the savage bull' (V.4.43). Benedick, by urging Don Pedro, 'thou art sad, get thee a wife' and concluding with a self-parodic *double-entendre*, 'there is no staff more reverend than one tipped with horn' (V.4. 114–16), bears witness to the capacity of requited love to overcome jealousy and suspicion.

The play pivots on honour – Don John's slander and Hero's disgrace and redemption. Messina's social code justifies Claudio in publicly insulting Hero and her father. Don Pedro jokes that Benedick has expended his sexual energy in Venice with Claudio his boon companion – 'Cupid spent all his quiver' (I.1.201). The sexual standard is double. Beatrice's virginity is not in doubt. Claudio has acquired 'much honour' (I.1.8) with his valour; allegiance to social superiors is also required. Woman's honour is predicated upon virginity before marriage and her subservience to man.

Beatrice has the most vigilant sense of honour. In friendship and love, honour demands absolute loyalty: Hero's dishonour she makes Benedick swear to extirpate as if it were her own. Don John and his followers are without honour: their word cannot be trusted, their ties are mercenary and self-interest their motive.

Honour is problematic. Beatrice exposes the gap between illusions of honour and reality. Her attack upon Claudio after his denunciation exposes the heartlessness and hypocrisy of his code of honour, which he invokes to mask conflicting emotions and promote male privilege. She cuts through his cant about deceitful appearances with trenchant realism: 'Is a not proved in the height a villain, that hath slandered, scorned, dishonoured my kinswoman!

Oh that I were a man!' (IV.1.291–2). She attacks Benedick's tentativeness, 'You dare easier be friends with me, than fight with mine enemy' (IV.1. 288–9), challenging the male solidarity central to the code of honour with reciprocity and sexual equality. She puts mutual feeling before fixed standards of conduct. She herself has defied the role Hero so willingly adopted: she assumes male dominance; instead of repressing or masking her feelings, she proclaims them and demands action upon them. By taking up the challenge of a dominant woman, Benedick courageously follows his conscience, not a code, and grows in moral stature

Honour remains under attack until the end, even though Don Pedro and Claudio do penance for their error. Their redemption is only partial. Claudio is flippant about marriage and Don Pedro is excluded from it.

SLANDER

Slander is abhorrent in Shakespeare's plays. In *Much Ado* the preponderance of spying, eavesdropping, gossip and misprision make slander inevitable. In the opening scene, Claudio's feats and his uncle's tearful response to them are reported. Beatrice extracts from the messenger a report of Benedick's performance in battle, Claudio reports his love to Benedick, who passes it on to Don Pedro, who offers to impersonate him in order to win his lady's affections. Within two scenes, Antonio and Borachio have misreported Don Pedro's designs upon Hero. Borachio's wooing Margaret in Hero's guise can be seen as a distortion of Don Pedro's disguised wooing of Hero, issuing from a similar compulsion and insecurity in a society where the appearance of honour is vigilantly enforced.

Unlike misunderstanding and misreport, the slander of Hero is deliberate and malicious. The masked ball ought to have taught Claudio to distrust Don John whose whispered warning of Don Pedro's treachery proved false. As soon as Claudio's engagement to Hero is announced, Don John's plot is concocted, which suggests that suspicion and fear are the other side of Claudio's idealisation. In Messina sexual relations are complicated by conventions and illusion. Benedick clings to an antique ideal of heroism. Truth

CHECK THE BOOK

Karen Newman traces the parallel treatment of slander in 'Mistaking', in Harold J. Bloom, ed., 1988, pp. 123–5 & 131–2.

becomes relative and elastic. Claudio and Don Pedro believe Don John before sifting the evidence. By shamming 'zeal' for 'his brother's honour' and 'his friend's reputation ... cozened with the semblance of a maid' (II.2.27–9), professing abhorrence and shame, using the **euphemistic** 'disloyal' and a blatant appeal to their status as gentlemen, Don John has Claudio vowing to 'shame her' in church with Don Pedro's backing, 'I'll join with thee' (III.2. 91–4).

Margaret keeps honour menacingly in the air: sex is honourable in marriage, she insists. The gravity of the slander is increased by the church setting, Claudio's image of the rotten orange, the three men ganging up on the one woman in **blank verse** and the malice of Don John's mock regret, 'pretty lady, I am sorry for your much misgovernment' (IV.1.91–2). Claudio's **oxymoron**, 'Thou pure impiety, and impious purity' (IV.1. 97), **ironically** emphasises the untruthfulness of the slander, which instantly divides a now murderous father and swooning daughter and Benedick and his friends, so ingrained are images of female duplicity and corruption.

In Messina the only antidote to slander is another fraud, the false report of Hero's death. More honourable men than Claudio and Don Pedro would have interpreted her death as the mark of innocence. Slander is a lie that will out so long as society insists upon a rigid ideal that conceals the truth.

GENDER

The controversial treatment of gender issues in *Much Ado* would have been central to its impact on Elizabethan audiences familiar with an extensive literature on the role of women. Independent, assertive, unruly women commanded attention on stage; the traditional pattern of feminine behaviour was under strain. Women were supposed to be silent, gentle, passive and submissive but Queen Elizabeth I herself projected an ambiguous male-female identity. The erosion of traditional gender ideologies created anxieties about the subversion of the social order. Loquacious, insubordinate, independent women were regarded with interest and suspicion. Comedy was a way of exploring such anxieties and diffusing them with laughter.

CHECK THE BOOK

George Brandes, in John Russell Brown, 1979, refers to the slanderer, Don John, as 'mere, unmixed evil', 'an ill-conditioned, base and tiresome scoundrel, pp. 41–2.

In the patriarchal society of *Much Ado* conventional codes of honour, camaraderie and a sense of superiority to women regulate masculine loyalties. Although female inconstancy is presumed, Balthasar's song deconstructs it and the fraud of men is dramatised in Claudio's ruthless treatment of Hero. Beatrice disrupts the conventional gender polarities, urging Hero to defy her father and putting Benedick on his mettle, although her role is ambiguous as she also yearns to exercise male power to avenge Hero. Benedick voices the traditional patriarchal ideology through his misogynist critique of woman's biting tongue and sexual lightness. Yet he breaks with his comrades when Hero is slandered and allies himself with Beatrice. He and Beatrice adopt an equivocal position in relation to the romantic conventions: they profess disdain and then submit to them.

Shakespearean men are flawed with pride; his women are capable of enduring love. His heroines often unite harmoniously the strengths commonly associated with one sex or the other – assertive but not aggressive, independent but not insular, erotic but not sensual, warm-hearted but without sentimentality, rational but sympathetic. Although *Much Ado* may lack a female exemplar of moral virtue, it almost champions sexual equality and female liberation. It is the least feminine of the comedies; the conventional heroine remains silent and the unconventional refuses to 'cry Heigh for a husband' (II.1.242–3). She does succumb to love but immediately assumes a dominant male role in demanding Claudio's death.

In the first three scenes, male characters continually put the female down. Leonato orders Hero to prepare to accept whoever courts her. Her duty is to 'be ruled by your father' (II.1.38), or, as Beatrice puts it, 'to make curtsy, and, say, father, as it please you' (II.1. 39–40), adding subversively, 'let him be a handsome fellow, or else make another curtsy and say, father, as it please me' (II.1. 40–1). Conventionally submissive, Hero refrains from answering.

Don Pedro claims that his motive for match-making is benevolent – Beatrice and Benedick are well-suited. It might also be a ploy to bring a critic of male privilege into line with the conventional patriarchal arrangement. Equally, although Benedick comments

CHECK THE BOOK

Harry Berger discloses the complications gender stereotypes create for male and female characters in 'Sexual and Family Politics', Harold Bloom, ed., 1988, pp. 21–37.

with neurotic repetitiveness, on female sexual lightness, he is endowing women with extraordinary power. So circumscribed by convention are married women that sexual infidelity would appear to be their only route to self-assertion in marriage.

Men are dominant, Claudio in war and romantic love, Don Pedro in arranging his friends' affairs and Benedick in championing the soldier's life and the sexual conquest of women. They cannot, therefore, know and empathise with women. Claudio denounces Hero, ironically, for not appearing to be all she seemed, an impossibility anyway, since he had idealised her. Female roles in Messina are circumscribed – virgin, wife and mother, or whore.

Beatrice has been the favourite of audiences, whether laughed at or with for transgressing the gender code to scold dominant man or for abandoning her pose of disdain and melting into a wife. Beatrice jokes about stuffing, being put down to become the mother of fools and even taking up the running joke on horns. In her wit she enters the male domain, not concealing her knowledge of sexual love and infidelity, though confident herself in the integrity of her own heart and the wholesomeness of her desires. She is not self-effacing; conversation revolves around her. Her courage in standing up for herself in an awkwardly dependent social position is laudable. She offends against propriety with a genteel charm. Benedick complains that her words can 'stab' (II.1.187) and once she launches an attack, she is inexorable and holds nothing back. This is a feature of her warm heart, as we see in her tears at Hero's suffering and her enlisting Benedick's support. She deplores the decline of the heroic ideal and condemns in her male peers the discrepancy between pretension and performance, such as the heroic Claudio's ignoble slander. The male ambiance of the play questions assumptions of male privilege and superiority.

Love and marriage are not in themselves deprecated. Beatrice, who in the opening scene beat the messenger verbally into submission, is tricked into loving the disdained misogynist. He, a notorious womaniser, conjures up a debased image of woman. A man's man, he makes casual references to whoring, the pleasures of drink, the hunt and war while making slighting reference to the straitjacket of

QUESTION

Is Shakespeare defeatist or conservative in his presentation of the situation of women?

marriage. Beatrice is no more flattering in her depiction of the dullness of contemporary man. Marriage, she proclaims, is conceived in lust, 'hot and hasty', born into conventions and restrictions, 'full of state and ancientry', and ends in deathly boredom, 'till he sink into his grave' (II.1.54–7).

Nevertheless, Beatrice and Benedick are brought into a jolly, fruitful if not peaceable union. Celibacy is not upheld, since, as Benedick puts it, 'the world must be peopled' (II.3.197), and therefore compromise of one's own desire with the opposite sex is necessary. In their mutual commitment, they offer a viable alternative to the dull conventionality of Hero's and Claudio's relationship. The power of love is demonstrated first in his conversion by hearsay and then by his willingness to sacrifice male solidarity for Beatrice's love. Her demand that he kill Claudio questions male dominance but affirms the fixed code of honour, since he is to avenge his fiancée's cousin's dishonour. Yet the relationship Beatrice requires is rooted in passionate mutual commitment which transcends gender limitations: 'You dare easier be friends with me than fight with mine enemy' (IV.1.288–9). Claudio's solidarity with Don Pedro had taken precedence over his attachment to Hero, whom, in an age when 'manhood is melted into curtsies' (IV.1.304), he can disgrace with impunity. By allying himself with Beatrice through fellow-feeling rather than form, he acts from sympathy rather than principle and attains heroic stature himself.

Beatrice will not let habit deaden their marriage. The 'merry war' (I.1.45) implies a questioning involvement in each other's inner life, an acknowledgement of the antagonism innate in any sexual relationship, respect for each other's independence and a belief in action. That they have been fooled into love is immaterial. Their union is a way of living with and transcending the gender stereotypes of their society.

NOSTALGIA

From the moment the messenger informs Leonato of Claudio's glorious feats in the recent war, *Much Ado* abounds in references to the past and the passing of time. This creates a lingering nostalgia for another and better age, which the prominent contrast between

CHECK THE BOOK

Barbara Everett argues that *Much Ado* is concerned with the 'mundane' in love and that it is the first play in which the differences of male and female worlds are prominent and the female predominates, see John Russell Brown, ed., 1979, p. 95.

the elderly and youthful characters strengthens, making the reconciliations of the final act more momentous.

Beatrice and Benedick dwell on the past, recent and remote, actual and legendary. She inveighs against the hypocrisy of men who swagger like classical heroes and pretend to an honour their action does not support. Her prejudice is confirmed when Hero is denounced. Her **oxymoron**, 'valiant dust' (II.1.44), juxtaposes pretence and reality. Benedick's recollection of his military past contains a spark of antique glory. He contrasts its manly simplicity with effeminate romantic love: 'he was wont to speak plain and to the purpose (like an honest man and a soldier) and now is he turned orthography' (II.3.15–16). Contrasted with a soldier's freedom and adventure – the hunt, womanising, target shooting, drinking – are domestic boredom and servitude, 'thrust thy neck into a yoke, wear the print of it, and sigh away Sundays' (I.1.8–9).

Beatrice and Benedick are energetic social critics. They yearn for past glory, which is the standpoint of their cutting **satiric** humour. Through the Watch wider satiric comment is made on the degeneracy of the age – the worship of fashion, the arrogance of power, the decay of morals.

The 'merry war' (I.1.45) between Beatrice and Benedick is playful and diverting, unlike the real pain which Claudio inflicts upon Hero in the name of honour. In their witty phrases, insults and ripostes a delight in the shaping of the language takes the sting from its tail. Their language roots them firmly in the present. When they confess their love for each other Benedick begins ironically, unable to take himself entirely seriously as a lover: is not a lover a fictional construction, he appears to inquire, required to behave in absurd, predictable ways? Therefore, he asks Beatrice, only half seriously, what wonders he, as gallant lover, can perform for her. Her 'Kill Claudio' (IV.l. 279) takes him aback, therefore, as it exacts commitment to an heroic ideal – protection of the weak by the strong, avenging dishonour. Both, through their nostalgia for the whole-heartedness of the past, commit themselves to action in the present, which gives their love vitality and their commitment to each other meaning.

> **CONTEXT**
>
> By hinting at the former existence of an ideal world from which society has decayed, pastoral comedy, present in *The Winter's Tale, As You Like It* and *Cymbeline*, tends to be nostalgic.

The roughness with which Beatrice exacts the promise and Benedick challenges Claudio and repudiates Don Pedro bespeaks their sincerity. Otherwise, their language has the wit and style of those removed from the stresses of life, steeped in the literature of the past. 'Is not that strange?' Benedick asks rhetorically as he confesses his love (IV.1.259–60) and 'for which of my bad parts didst thou first fall in love with me?' he enquires once they are betrothed. He savours her metaphor when she in turn asks, 'for which of my good parts did you first suffer love for me' (V.3.44–8). They agree finally to love each other 'no more than reason' (V.4.74) reconciled to the changes of time and nature, since 'man is a giddy thing' (V.4.104).

Their wit has been softened, not lost. Although the code of honour has not entirely been rejected, since the romantic lovers do in the end marry once Hero is vindicated, it has been challenged and renewed. Claudio's and Leonato's insensitivity has exposed the destructiveness of a nostalgic adherence to an archaic code. Beatrice and Benedick love with an intensity they imagined was an aspect of former times. Although their literary style both establishes a continuity with the past and detaches them from their own passions, their involvement in the present is enhanced.

NATURE

Much Ado is an indoor play of wit, deception and slander. For Benedick, the law imposes the dullness of marriage upon man and woman against their nature and the wife takes it out on the husband by making him a cuckold. For Beatrice, a preoccupation with death arises from her entrapment within a court whose practices she cannot admire. The play is claustrophobic. Spies are hidden in its many rooms. Scenes of togetherness in one room are followed by those of conspiracy in another, which emphasises human isolation and vulnerability.

Claudio's conventional lover's hyperbole to Hero indicates his estrangement from his natural desires. The denunciation scene takes place at the altar of a chapel, which exaggerates the enormous power of institutions and conventions over the individual, whose emotions it numbs and distorts.

QUESTION

Some critics have claimed that *Much Ado About Nothing* is a simple romantic comedy; others have found it as a sharp attack on superficial society. What are your views? In your answer define 'romantic comedy' and 'social criticism' and comment on what the play suggests about the importance of romantic love.

Nature continued

A feature of Benedick's and Beatrice's wit is the obscene *double-entendre*. Through their anomalous roles as celibate disdainers of love and marriage, they voice the fear and distaste for the opposite sex so evidently latent in Claudio and also remind the audience of the element in love occluded by the romantic conventions of Messina. In earthy, bawdy dialogue with Hero on her wedding day and with Benedick after he has vowed to challenge Claudio, Margaret adopts a more obscene version of Beatrice's bawdy wit, appropriate to a servant and mistress, less constrained by social conventions than her betters. She speaks for the democracy of shameless sexual desire, 'Is not marriage honourable in a beggar?' (III.2.22–3).

The Watch represent the common people of Messina. They work by night, which corresponds with their dim intellects. Whereas the aristocracy speak a highly artificial language, and strictly observe external signs and symbols, the Watch speak a murky language, much closer to nature, in which the signs are unclear and distinctions blurred. That the Watch solves Don John's crime invests hope in nature, whose beneficence arranges matters for the best, in spite of human interference.

CONTEXT

Comedies like *A Midsummer's Night's Dream* and *As You Like It* in which the green world is more prominent are more light-hearted and festive.

Although nature is present only obliquely, Claudio falls in love with Hero outside Leonato's house and Beatrice and Benedick in the orchard on an evening 'hushed on purpose to grace harmony' (II.3.31). The beauty of Hero's mind emerges from her poetic evocation of 'the pleachèd bower, / Where honeysuckles ripened by the sun,/ Forbid the sun to enter' (III.1.7–9), 'where Beatrice like a lapwing runs / Close by the ground' (III.1. 24–5). Musically, Balthasar creates the mood with 'Sigh no more' (II.3.53), a melancholy lyric counselling women to resign themselves to male inconstancy. Although the song foreshadows Claudio's inconstancy and reflects upon Benedick's reported womanising, female inconstancy is in the foreground, primarily in Benedick's obsession with their lightness but also in Claudio's fear of Hero's bewitching power and in Don John's slander. The natural images of sand and sea are used to represent the constant ebb and flow of human desire which music and the sweetness of nature prompt.

Night is the setting of Don John's deception, ruthless daylight of Hero's denunciation and night of Claudio's dirge of expiation in the graveyard. The penance fulfilled, the torches are put out and light, harbinger of dawn and symbol of hope, appears in the sky. 'The wolves have preyed', Don Pedro comments, referring to the evil which has destroyed Hero. 'And look,' he adds, 'the gentle day / Before the wheels of Phoebus, round about / Dapples the drowsy east with spots of grey' (V.4.25–7). The verse naturalises Claudio's aggression. The daylight signifies his reconciliation with his darker side. In *Much Ado* nature thus maintains a subtle presence in the cycle of day and night, symbolic of truth and falsehood, goodness and evil, and in the sense of the urgency of time. This implies a necessary correlation between the rhythms of nature and the operation of the human spirit, particularly in love, which establishes a harmonious relationship between man and woman and within the individual between his passion and reason.

STRUCTURE

Much Ado About Nothing is written with extreme economy. In seventeen scenes with only four settings – outside and inside Leonato's house, in the orchard and in a chapel, all in Messina – a sense of ample space and gracious if urgent time is created. The characters form balanced groups of twos and threes. The symmetry of the plot structure is suggestive of a masquerade or a dance, appropriate in a play dominated by spying and deception and in which harmony is established through love.

The opening scene in which Claudio reveals his love to his friend and patron, who promises to promote it, is followed by two scenes in which spies misreport that confession to their patrons. In that opening scene, there are two set pieces of formally polite conversation, one of which Beatrice interrupts, the other Benedick, establishing the affinity underlying their antagonism.

On the evening of the soldiers' arrival Hero and Claudio are betrothed at one dance. Benedick calls for another dance as the curtain falls. Songs at two crucial points in the play create rhythm.

 CHECK THE BOOK
Pamela Mason, 1992, argues that the masked ball demonstrated the 'independence of mind and spirit' in Beatrice and Benedick most clearly delineated in the church scene, p. 19.

'Sigh no more' (II.3.53) foreshadows Claudio's inconstancy and creates a conducive atmosphere for turning Beatrice and Benedick into lovers. 'Pardon goddess of the night' (V.3.12), an apology for that inconstancy, heralds the dawn of renewed love and reconciliation.

At the masked ball, Claudio's anxiety about Don Pedro's wooing on his behalf is intensified, once jestingly by Benedick and once malevolently by Don John, just as later a benevolent deception unites Beatrice and Benedick and malevolent divides Hero and Claudio. **Soliloquies** before and after Benedick's gulling create a comic frame. In the first he questions his capacity for love; in the second he vows to dive madly into it. Until the gulling in the orchard, scenes within the house, owing to Don John's machinations, become increasingly claustrophobic. Dialogue between Margaret and Hero and a soliloquy chiming with Benedick devoting himself to love frame Beatrice's gulling. Comic scenes follow: first Benedick, then Beatrice, are teased for love sickness. Don John's plot abruptly snaps the comic mood which returns with the introduction of the Watch. A scene of gentle banter before the wedding and a short comic scene in which the Watch fail in their attempt to inform Leonato about the plot, deepen the pathos. The contrastingly long denunciation scene divides neatly into the attack on Hero, the Friar's remedy, and the coming together of Beatrice and Benedick, who promises to challenge Claudio. The Watch's farcical examination of Borachio and Conrade underlines the injustice of Hero's trial. Farce continues when Antonio and Leonato almost come to blows with Claudio and Don Pedro. Benedick has challenged Claudio, the male bond severed, as the Watch enter and the truth comes to light. Claudio and Don Pedro make their public shows of grief and apology after which the weddings soon take place with the play ending in joyful reconciliation.

CHECK THE BOOK

Sherman Hawkins distinguishes *Much Ado* from green world comedies constructed around two settings. The closed world setting of Messina is 'a symbol for the human heart', see John Russell Brown, ed., 1979, p. 57.

LANGUAGE AND IMAGERY

Three quarters of *Much Ado* are written in a prose similar in structure and diction to the English spoken today. Prose suits the earthy realism of the principal wits, Beatrice and Benedick, upon whose quick, apparently spontaneous repartee the comedy depends.

The characters in the romantic plot, principally Hero and Claudio, are apt to declaim in verse, which underlines, by contrast, the artificiality and ideality of their sentiments. In the first scene, for example, the dialogue, even of the sententious messenger and Leonato, is in prose until Claudio is left alone with Don Pedro to confess his love. His lyricism – 'thronging soft and delicate desires' (I.1.227) – becomes the more elevated by contrast with Benedick's former down-to-earth mockery, 'Would you buy her, that you enquire after her?' (I.1.133). However affecting Claudio's sentiments, the formality of the verse hints at the underlying illusion.

Hero's extreme reticence until her betrothal creates her mystique – she connives in Claudio's idealisation. Out of the public eye, she speaks in verse with a refined wit indicative of an inner beauty and intelligence which her social role, as Claudio's fiancée, leads her to suppress:

> And bid her steal into the pleachèd bower,
> Where honeysuckles ripened by the sun,
> Forbid the sun to enter: like favourites,
> Made proud by princes   (III.1.7–10)

The dignity of her verse exacerbates the injustice of her disgrace and darkens the comedy.

Benedick attains verse only briefly when he pledges his support for the Friar's scheme (IV.1). He fails miserably to indite a love sonnet to Beatrice, which seems right, as both are too realistic to believe for long in romantic illusions. Unlike Benedick, Beatrice is so transformed from Lady Disdain by love that, after the eavesdropping, in her soliloquy, she does dedicate herself to requiting Benedick in verse of alternately rhyming lines of iambic pentameter. Indeed, the entire gulling of Beatrice in verse, unlike Benedick's in prose, highlights implicit gender differences.

The deepest and highest sentiments of the play are expressed in blank verse. In IV.1 Claudio switches from prose to verse once he has begun Hero's denunciation. Paradox, metaphor and rhetorical structures endow his verse with the same ritualistic quality as the

> **CONTEXT**
>
> In his most romantic tragedy Romeo and Juliet's lyrical outpourings of love are contrasted with the realistic wit of Mercutio and the bawdy humour of the nurse.

wedding ceremony and communicate the strength of his disillusionment. Whereas Beatrice and Benedick had shown off their wit by playfully engaging in a war of words for the entertainment of the company, here the formality and complexity of the blank verse underlines the discrepancy between illusion and reality and the pain deception causes:

> Oh Hero! What a hero hadst thou been,
> If half thy outward graces had been placed
> About thy thoughts and counsels of thy heart?   (IV.1.92–5)

Leonato's tirade and the Friar's consolation are also in verse and only when Beatrice is left on the stage alone with Benedick is there a return to prose, where again the simplicity of the language conveys the honesty of their feelings: 'Lady Beatrice, have you wept all this while?' (IV.1.248).

In V.1 the alternation of prose and verse is as striking. The verse with which Antonio attempts to console Leonato is maintained through the conflict with Claudio and Don Pedro. Only when Benedick enters to throw down a challenge to Claudio is the dialogue in prose, which continues until the Watch has revealed the truth about Hero's slander. Leonato returns declaiming in verse, to which Claudio and Don Pedro reply contritely in kind. The scene ends with the garbled prose of the Watch, which steers the play towards the joyful reconciliations of the final scene.

CHECK THE BOOK

John Traugott, 'Creating a Rational Rinaldo', in Harold Bloom, ed., 1988, pp. 39–62, attributes the realism and poetry in the language to the blending of the genres of romance and comedy.

The prose is varied according to character. The play opens with a **euphuistic** exchange between Leonato and the messenger, in which feelings are elevated and depersonalised through the use of elaborate syntax, **metaphor**, balance and **antithesis**. 'He hath indeed better bettered expectation than you must expect of me to tell you how' (I.1.12–13). This Beatrice pricks with the directness of one question, 'I pray you, is Signor Mountato returned from the wars or no?' (I.1.23), as does Benedick, Don Pedro and Leonato with his teasing, 'were you in doubt, sir, that you asked her' (I.1.79).

Exaggeration, imaginative vitality and prolixity are the signal features of Beatrice's and Benedick's prose. It is also classically and proverbially allusive, indicative of a broad experience and education and abounds in imagery. Both have a fondness for the martial and heroic image, which Benedick exploits in a self-aggrandising fashion and Beatrice to mock male pretensions. They trace insults with animal imagery. Their use of classical myth and imagery conjures up a more heroic age against which the present appears shabby. Benedick adopts images of the hunt and of sexual aggression, Beatrice references to age, death and decay. Clothing imagery identifies the importance of deception. Although the interiors of Leonato's house come to symbolise separateness, alienation and distrust, natural imagery keeps in the audience's minds the proximity of human warmth.

Beatrice and Benedick tend in their prose towards self-dramatisation and self-exploration. One idea, feeling or image is associated with another until the original is lost in whimsy and sentiment, which is the antithesis of the rigid code of honour by which Messina operates. Leonato's remark that Beatrice is too 'curst' (II.1.14–20) to get a husband kindles in her a reference first to cows, then to apes, followed by Saint Peter, a 'cloc of wayward marl' and finally to the three types of dances with which she illustrates the normal course of marriage (II.1.45–57). When Benedick complains at the masked ball that Beatrice has 'misused me past the endurance of a block' (II.1.181), his range of allusion is breathtaking, as he ends with allusions to mythology and the Scriptures, which suggest that his pleasure in his own wit far exceeds his displeasure at her mockery. The rhythm of the prose arises from this rapid association of ideas and the underlying spirit of enquiry.

By contrast, the language of villainy, particularly that of Don John, though no less rhetorical, is stiffly formal and halting. There is a similar egotism, but without the playfulness, which makes it cold and aggressive. Whereas references to nature lend the wits' speech an airy naturalness, that of the villains is claustrophobic.

The language of the Watch provides a distorted image of the language of the court and an antidote to the stiltedress of Don John. Whereas the pace of the repartee is swift, the images plentiful and

CHECK THE BOOK
Roger Sales, 1987, offers a detailed analysis of Dogberry's comic language and his thematic and moral role.

'Song, dance and farce in *Much Ado About Nothing* merely serve to bring into prominence its overriding sadness.' How helpful do you find this view to your under-standing of the play and its effects?

vivid and the word play precise, versatile and clever, the Watch speak with halting deliberation, uncertain of their grammar and vocabulary, without playfulness, allusiveness or wit, and the comedy arises not from their ability to play upon words but from their misunderstanding of their meaning. So literal are they that they take the difficult word, 'deformed' (III.3.103), for an incarnation of sin, which the play suggests, **ironically**, is not too wide of the mark.

PART FOUR

CRITICAL HISTORY

STAGE HISTORY

There is strong evidence of the popularity of *Much Ado*, especially the characters of Beatrice and Benedick, from its first performance until the closing of the theatres in 1648. Little is known of its theatrical history from the restoration of 1660 until 1721, when it was advertised as not having been performed for thirty years. Garrick, the renowned actor, first played Benedick in 1748 and performed it frequently to acclaim until his retirement in 1776. The famous Beatrice of Mrs Jordan of the late eighteenth century was hearty and jolly; Fanny Kemble's of the late 1820s refined and generous. Henry Irving and Ellen Terry played Benedick and Beatrice in a grand production that ran for 212 performances in 1882 and 1883. Ellen Terry's Beatrice was famous for 'gaiety and humour, grace and vivacity, tenderness, dignity and deep feeling' (Gordon Crosse, *Shakespeare Playgoing 1890–1952*, Mowbray, 1953, p.15). Forbes-Robertson played Claudio in the production with a 'consuming and insanely suspicious jealousy' to explain his offensive conduct. In 1903 Gordon Craig revolutionised the setting. He made it bare and impressionistic by widening the light that illuminated the colours of a huge cross in the church scene. Beerbohm Tree's production of 1905 revived the grandiose Victorian style.

The play has continued to be revived regularly in London and Stratford. John Gielgud's production at Stratford in 1949, deemed particularly outstanding, was revived in 1950, 1952, 1955 and 1959. Set amid a period of restraint and rationing, it offered luxurious escapism into a world of fantasy. The sets were opulent, with a fairytale quality. Hero and Claudio were impetuous and inexperienced, star-crossed children victimised by Don John. In the heavily naturalistic church scene, organ music and many guests highlighted its public nature. Don John's movement with a hat, noted by Benedick, when Don Pedro calls Hero a 'common stale' (IV.1.59) reinforced his villainy. Claudio's frenzied movement

CHECK THE FILM

The Elizabethan world of competing London theatre companies and impoverished actors is vigorously brought to life on screen in John Madden's 1998 film, *Shakespeare in Love*.

QUESTION

In what ways is the gap between appearance and reality explored in *Much Ado About Nothing?*

towards and away from Hero indicated his internal conflict and distress. Of his two leading ladies, Diana Wynward played Beatrice as a grand lady and Peggy Ashcroft as a cheeky spinster who is unlikely to marry because she is too free with her tongue. His own Benedick evolved from a courtier and dandy into a bluff, uncouth soldier contemptuous of society.

Zeffirelli's National Theatre production of 1965 set the play in late nineteenth-century Messina with heavy Mafia overtones. 'The sweating sunblown splendour and squalor of the real Mediterranean' implied by the setting lent Claudio's accusation credibility. Zeffirelli enlivened the play with farcical stage business. Robert Graves reworked the text, 300 of his lines being adapted to clarify or explain what he regarded as ambiguous. Human statues freezing and moving on stage contributed to a carnival atmosphere. Even Derek Jacobi's Don John was comic – petulant, neurotic and hyperactive. Dogberry had a thick Italian accent and Verges rode a bicycle. The successful church scene began comically, which made Claudio's rejection intensely shocking. Margaret's presence on stage heightened tension: her gestures showed that she realised what was happening but dared not speak on such a grave occasion. The savage force of Beatrice's 'Kill Claudio!' stunned the audience and Benedick, whose reply, 'not for the wide world' (IV.1.279–80) was whispered. When he offered his hand, she removed his dagger and placed it in his hand. Albert Finney's strutting Don Pedro controlled the closing moments, looking up at the single lamp illuminating the stage just before the final note of music, bowing and plunging the auditorium into darkness, encapsulating 'the balance between absurd, anarchic comedy and bitter, vehement energy' (Pamela Mason, *Much Ado About Nothing: Text and Performance*, Macmillan, 1992, p. 55).

Trevor Nunn's 1968 production was a reaction against Zeffirelli's flamboyance. The setting was late Renaissance, the set enclosed, the costumes subdued. There were significant cuts, such as Antonio's insult of Claudio's youth, which made him more culpable and moved the play closer to tragedy. The masque was military and sombre. The Hero–Claudio plot took precedence, she a young girl adored by her father, Claudio an adolescent with rapid mood swings. He pushed Hero violently towards Leonato in the church scene, which clashed with his former passivity. Hero's vulnerability was emphasised by a too large, doll-like dress and Benedick's affinity with the Friar in their white habits. The scene had started formally, the stage cleared in chaos and confusion leaving Benedick and Beatrice isolated and remote. Restrained movement followed by kneeling accompanied their professions of love, the solemnity of which was shattered with 'Kill Claudio!' shouted at full volume with a break in Beatrice's voice, to which Benedick gently replied that he could not.

John Barton's 1976 Stratford production was an attempt to create an Elizabethan stage for a setting in colonial India. Within Leonato's household Beatrice occupied a busy, subservient role. The atmosphere was of an officers' mess in a male-dominated society, the characters' sense of superiority reinforced by the ethos of the public school and military academy. To them everything was a game, Don John's plot being concocted during a cricket match. Thus Claudio had to show publicly that he rejected Hero for the sake of his and the regiment's honour. Lack of the physical prowess and arrogance of the others excluded Don John and made him a comic figure, his 'I cannot hide what I am' (I.3.10) arousing pity rather than scorn. The Watch were played as Indian natives, which gave credence to their struggles with the language, and their slow movement contributed to the impression of oppressive heat. A spirited Hero responded to Claudio's accusation with outraged anger. Beatrice started to sweep up scattered flowers after the denunciation, a woman who used her chores to repress sexual and social frustration, and her 'Kill Claudio!' was a peremptory demand forced from the lips of a tiny, crouched figure. Although Claudio's penitence was shown to be sincere, Beatrice and Benedick, whose play it was, by refusing to follow the others off stage at the end, remained to assert their individuality.

A 1981 National Theatre production was praised for being 'exquisitely non-committal'. Terry Hands directed a 1982 production comparable with Gielgud's in its visual charm. A set with mirrors was the narcissistic setting for a self-absorbed and vain society of the Caroline age, although soft lighting preserved a festive

QUESTION

Much Ado About Nothing suggests that the battle of the sexes is eternal because it will always be a man's world.' How helpful do you find this view in understanding the relations of the sexes in the play?

joy. In 1988 the Renaissance Theatre Company's production created a warm, cosy atmosphere with Leonato an affectionate and adored father and Beatrice a happy family member. Beatrice and Benedick were youthful and serious. Her proposal to Don Pedro was in earnest, a search for relief from the disturbance the engagement of Hero had caused her. The overhearing scene was rich in beauty and pathos, Benedick's response deeply felt but reluctantly admitted. Margaret's role was clearly defined as a sexually experienced woman who could play games with Borachio through the window without anticipating harm to anyone. She was worldly wise and slightly coarse, rather than perceptive, and the exclusiveness of the wedding explained her absence. In the church scene, Benedick's 'This looks not like a nuptial' (IV.1.62) was an angry rebuke accompanied by shaking Claudio, who wept when he later discovered his error. Hero wailed during the denunciation and her father's attack was unbearable to her.

QUESTION

'Conflict – of gender, age and class – not reconciliation, is the lasting impression this play leaves.' How helpful do you find this view to uyour understanding of *Much Ado About Nothing* and its effects?

Bill Alexander's Royal Shakespeare Company production of 1990 established the civilised restraint of Messina society with clipped, maze-like hedges so useful in the overhearing scenes. As she actually fenced with Leonato as the curtain rose, Beatrice's cries of 'Oh God that I were a man' (IV.1.294) were anticipated. Benedick was presented as a clubbable, raffish eternal bachelor constantly wreathed in cigar smoke whose overhearing of Beatrice's love is an emotional shock from which he cannot recover. Don Pedro devised the overhearing scheme from a sense of responsibility and a relish in playing the voyeur. His use of sexual innuendo in the emphasis given to 'bosom', 'force' and 'amorous tale' (I.2.249–251) gave credence to Claudio's jealousy. Don John was played as a conventional villain of melodrama. Don Pedro was aghast when he learned what his brother had done and Benedick's 'get thee a wife' (V.4.115) at the end of the play became pointed.

The 1993 production mounted in London by Matthew Warchus balanced comedy with emphasis on the serious themes of deception and false appearance. The marquee-like set drew attention to artifice and theatricality. Benedick wore a blood-stained bandage which he took off to reveal no wound. Mark Rylance portrayed him as a nervous, insecure Ulsterman who hid his vulnerability behind a disagreeable mask. Janet McTeer's physically dominating Beatrice was in complete control as she delivered her witticisms like a fury. Little flashes of anxiety hinting at discomfort with her image prepared the audience for her conversion.

VIDEO AND FILM PRODUCTIONS

Much Ado was filmed by the BBC in 1984 directed by Stuart Burge. The setting was Mediterranean, costumes Renaissance with a hint of the Turkish. The couples of lovers were of the same age, Beatrice the strongest. The style was formal and courtly; the heavy-looking sets and the series of slow-moving tableaux sapped its vitality. Beatrice was presented as quick-witted, independent, sexually attractive and good-natured. She enjoyed making herself the centre of attention. Benedick was caustic or droll. In his dramatic change of heart, good use was made of close-ups to register his nervous vulnerability and sudden youthfulness.

Kenneth Branagh's film, released in 1993, exploited visual possibilities more fully. It reached a wider audience through its use of movie stars and general release in the cinema. It was shot on location in a Tuscan villa, with warm, panoramic shots of the house and surrounding countryside. The Italian setting created a viable context for the passions aroused by Don John's plot. Character and dialogue were naturalistic, but slow motion footage of galloping horsemen, mood and overhead shots signalled the artifice of the medium. Close-ups, creative backlighting, dissolve and montage effects brought out emotions and cuts between sequences intensified contrasts. Emma Thompson as Beatrice read the song 'Sigh no more' (II.3. 53) wistfully at the beginning, it was sung sadly in the garden and repeated triumphantly at the end, which placed gender issues at the centre. Beatrice was an assertive modern woman, confidently superior in the merry war. Branagh's Benedick was waggish, complacent and opinionated. Both were romantics at heart. Naked bodies, sensuous women bathing and dressing to prepare for the men's arrival and Margaret and Borachio copulating in a window made it a physical production. Prominence was given to the Hero–Claudio–Don John plot at the expense of the verbal

 **QUESTION**

'There are echoing ironies in the love plots.' Discuss Shakespeare's presentation of the contrasting relationships between Beatrice and Benedick and Hero and Claudio in the light of this comment.

CHECK THE NET

For information about the London reconstruction of Shakespeare's Globe, visit **http:// www. shakespeares-globe.org/**.

artifice with 500 lines cut. Rearrangement of events leading to Don John's deception darkened the plot line while cuts to Don Pedro's and Claudio's dialogue made them appear more serious and sincere. The dark elements of the play were accentuated to contrast with the light-hearted. The Watchmen were ruthless to their prisoners. At the end Don Pedro and Don John looked hatefully at each other before the final joyous dance and song.

WILLIAM SHAKESPEARE'S LIFE

There are no personal records of Shakespeare's life. Official documents and occasional references to him by contemporary dramatists enable us to draw the main outline of his public life, but his private life remains hidden. Although not at all unusual for a writer of his time, this lack of first-hand evidence has tempted many to read his plays as personal records and to look in them for clues to Shakespeare's character and convictions. The results are unconvincing, partly because Renaissance art was not subjective or designed primarily to express its creator's personality, and partly because the drama of any period is very difficult to read biographically. Except when plays are written by committed dramatists to promote social or political causes (as by Shaw or Brecht), it is all but impossible to decide who amongst the variety of fictional characters in a drama represents the dramatist, or which of the various and often conflicting points of view expressed is authorial.

What we do know can be quickly summarised. Shakespeare was born into a well-to-do family in the market town of Stratford-upon-Avon in Warwickshire, where he was baptised, in Holy Trinity Church, on 26 April 1564. His father, John Shakespeare, was a prosperous glover and leather merchant who became a person of some importance in the town: in 1565 he was elected an alderman of the town, and in 1568 he became high bailiff (or mayor) of Stratford. In 1557 he had married Mary Arden. Their third child (of eight) and eldest son, William, learned to read and write at the primary (or 'petty') school in Stratford and then, it seems probable, attended the local grammar school, where he would have studied Latin, history, logic and rhetoric. In November 1582 William, then aged eighteen, married Anne Hathaway, who was twenty-six years old. They had a daughter, Susanna, in May 1583, and twins, Hamnet and Judith, in 1585.

CHECK THE BOOK

There are a number of biographies of Shakespeare – many of them very speculative – but the most authoritative is still Samuel Schoenbaum's *William Shakespeare: A Compact Documentary Life* (OUP, 1977).

CHECK THE NET

For information on Shakespeare's home town of Stratford-upon-Avon, including sites associated with the dramatist, visit **http://www. stratford.co.uk**, or **http://www. stratford-upon-avon.co.uk**.

Shakespeare next appears in the historical record in 1592 when he is mentioned as a London actor and playwright in a pamphlet by the dramatist Robert Greene. These 'lost years' 1585–92 have been the subject of much speculation, but how they were occupied remains as much a mystery as when Shakespeare left Stratford, and why. In his pamphlet, *Greene's Groatsworth of Wit*, Greene expresses to his fellow dramatists his outrage that the 'upstart crow' Shakespeare has the impudence to believe he 'is as well able to bombast out a blank verse as the best of you'. To have aroused this hostility from a rival, Shakespeare must, by 1592, have been long enough in London to have made a name for himself as a playwright. We may conjecture that he had left Stratford in 1586 or 1587.

During the next twenty years, Shakespeare continued to live in London, regularly visiting his wife and family in Stratford. He continued to act, but his chief fame was as a dramatist. From 1594 he wrote exclusively for the Lord Chamberlain's Men, which rapidly became the leading dramatic company and from 1603 enjoyed the patronage of James I as the King's Men. His plays were extremely popular and he became a shareholder in his theatre company. He was able to buy land around Stratford and a large house in the town, to which he retired in about 1611. He died there on 23 April 1616 and was buried in Holy Trinity Church on 25 April.

SHAKESPEARE'S DRAMATIC CAREER

CHECK THE NET

You can read Shakespeare's will in his own handwriting – and in modern transcription – online at the Public Records Office: **http://www.pro. gov.uk/ virtualmuseum** and search for 'Shakespeare'.

Between the late 1580s and 1613 Shakespeare wrote thirty-seven plays, and contributed to some by other dramatists. This was by no means an exceptional number for a professional playwright of the times. The exact date of the composition of individual plays is a matter of debate – the date of first performance is known for only a few plays – but the broad outlines of Shakespeare's dramatic career have been established. He began in the late 1580s and early 1590s by rewriting earlier plays and working with plotlines inspired by the Classics. He concentrated on comedies (such as *The Comedy of Errors*, 1590–4, which derived from the Latin playwright Plautus) and plays dealing with English history (such as the three parts of *Henry VI*, 1589–92), though he also tried his hand at bloodthirsty revenge tragedy (*Titus Andronicus*, 1592–3, indebted to both Ovid and Seneca). During the 1590s Shakespeare developed his expertise in these kinds of plays to write comic masterpieces such as *A Midsummer Night's Dream* (1594–5) and *As You Like It* (1599–1600) and history plays such as *Henry IV* (1596–8) and *Henry V* (1598–9).

As the new century begins a new note is detectable. Plays such as *Troilus and Cressida* (1601–2) and *Measure for Measure* (1603–4), poised between comedy and tragedy, evoke complex responses. Because of their generic uncertainty and ambivalent tone such works are sometimes referred to as 'problem plays', but it is tragedy which comes to dominate the extraordinary sequence of masterpieces: *Hamlet* (1600–1), *Othello* (1602–4), *King Lear* (1605–6), *Macbeth* (1605–6) and *Antony and Cleopatra* (1606).

In the last years of his dramatic career, Shakespeare wrote a group of plays of a quite different kind. These 'romances', as they are often called, are in many ways the most remarkable of all his plays. The group comprises *Pericles* (1608), *Cymbeline* (1609–11), *The Winter's Tale* (1610–11) and *The Tempest* (1610–11). These plays (particularly *Cymbeline*) reprise many of the situations and themes of the earlier dramas but in fantastical and exotic dramatic designs which, set in distant lands, covering large tracts of time and involving music, mime, dance and tableaux, have something of the qualities of masques and pageants. The situations which in the tragedies had led to disaster are here resolved: the great theme is restoration and reconciliation. Where in the tragedies Ophelia, Desdemona and Cordelia die, the daughters of these plays – Marina, Imogen, Perdita, Miranda – survive and are reunited with their parents and lovers.

THE TEXTS OF SHAKESPEARE'S PLAYS

Nineteen of Shakespeare's plays were printed during his lifetime in what are called 'quartos': books, each containing one play, and made up of sheets of paper each folded twice to make four leaves. Shakespeare, however, did not supervise their publication. This was not unusual. When a playwright sold a play to a dramatic company he sold his rights in it: copyright belonged to whoever had possession of an actual copy of the text, and consequently authors had no control over what happened to their work. Anyone who

CHECK THE FILM
There are lots of anachronisms and inaccuracies in *Shakespeare in Love* (1998) – that's half the fun of it – but its depiction of the hand-to-mouth world of the commercial theatre has something of the energy and edginess from which Shakespeare drew his artistic power.

CONTEXT
A quarto is a small format book, roughly equivalent to a modern paperback. Play texts in quarto form typically cost sixpence, as opposed to the cost of going to the theatre at a penny.

CONTEXT

Plays were not considered as serious literature in this period: when, in 1612, Sir Thomas Bodley was setting up his library in Oxford he instructed his staff not to buy any drama for the collection: 'haply [perhaps] some plays may be worthy the keeping, but hardly one in forty.'

could get hold of the text of a play might publish it if they wished. Hence, what found its way into print might be the author's copy, but it might be an actor's copy or prompt copy, perhaps cut or altered for performance; sometimes actors (or even members of the audience) might publish what they could remember of the text. Printers, working without the benefit of the author's oversight, introduced their own errors, through misreading the manuscript for example, and by 'correcting' what seemed to them not to make sense.

In 1623 John Heminges and Henry Condell, two actors in Shakespeare's company, collected together texts of thirty-six of Shakespeare's plays (*Pericles* was omitted) and published them in a large folio (a book in which each sheet of paper is folded once in half, to give two leaves). This, the First Folio, was followed by later editions in 1632, 1663 and 1685. Despite its appearance of authority, however, the texts in the First Folio still present many difficulties, for there are printing errors and confused passages in the plays, and its texts often differ significantly from those of the earlier quartos, when these exist.

Shakespeare's texts have, then, been through a number of intermediaries. We do not have the playwright's authority for any of his plays, and hence we cannot know exactly what it was that he wrote. Bibliographers, textual critics and editors have spent a great deal of effort on endeavouring to get behind the errors, uncertainties and contradictions in the available texts to recover the plays as Shakespeare originally wrote them. What we read is the result of these efforts. Modern texts are what editors have constructed from the available evidence: they correspond to no sixteenth- or seventeenth-century editions, and to no early performance of a Shakespeare play. Furthermore, these composite texts differ from each other, for different editors read the early texts differently and come to different conclusions. A Shakespeare text is an unstable and a contrived thing.

Often, of course, its judgements embody, if not the personal prejudices of the editor, then the cultural preferences of the time in which he or she was working. Growing awareness of this has led recent scholars to distrust the whole editorial enterprise and to repudiate the attempt to construct a 'perfect' text. Stanley Wells and Gary Taylor, the editors of the Oxford edition of *The Complete Works* (1988), point out that almost certainly the texts of Shakespeare's plays were altered in performance, and from one performance to another, so that there may never have been a single version. They note, too, that Shakespeare probably revised and rewrote some plays. They do not claim to print a definitive text of any play, but prefer what seems to them the 'more theatrical' version, and when there is a great difference between available versions, as with *King Lear*, they print two texts.

SHAKESPEARE AND THE ENGLISH RENAISSANCE

Shakespeare arrived in London at the very time that the Elizabethan period was poised to become the 'golden age' of English literature. Although Elizabeth reigned as queen from 1558 to 1603, the term 'Elizabethan' is used very loosely in a literary sense to refer to the period 1580 to 1625, when the great works of the age were produced. (Sometimes the later part of this period is distinguished as 'Jacobean', from the Latin form of the name of the king who succeeded Elizabeth, James I of England and VI of Scotland, who reigned from 1603 to 1625.) The poet Edmund Spenser heralded this new age with his pastoral poem *The Shepheardes Calender* (1579), and in his essay *An Apologie for Poetrie* (written about 1580, although not published until 1595) his friend Sir Philip Sidney championed the imaginative power of the 'speaking picture of poesy', famously declaring that 'Nature never set forth the earth in so rich a tapestry as divers poets have done ... Her world is brazen, the poet's only deliver a golden'.

Spenser and Sidney were part of that rejuvenating movement in European culture which since the nineteenth century has been known by the term 'Renaissance'. Meaning literally 'rebirth' it denotes a revival and redirection of artistic and intellectual endeavour which began in Italy in the fourteenth century with the poetry of Petrarch. It spread gradually northwards across Europe, and is first detectable in England in the early sixteenth century in

 CHECK THE NET

You can consult texts by Spenser and Sidney, and other contemporaries of Shakespeare, at Renascence Editions **http://www. uoregon.edu/ ~rbear/ren.htm**.

the writings of the scholar and statesman Sir Thomas More and in the poetry of Sir Thomas Wyatt and Henry Howard, Earl of Surrey. Its keynote was a curiosity in thought which challenged old assumptions and traditions. To the innovative spirit of the Renaissance, the preceding ages appeared dully unoriginal and conformist.

That spirit was fuelled by the rediscovery of many Classical texts and the culture of Greece and Rome. This fostered a confidence in human reason and in human potential which, in every sphere, challenged old convictions. The discovery of America and its peoples (Columbus had sailed in 1492) demonstrated that the world was a larger and stranger place than had been thought. The cosmological speculation of Copernicus (later confirmed by Galileo) that the sun, not the earth was the centre of our planetary system challenged the centuries-old belief that the earth and human beings were at the centre of the cosmos. The pragmatic political philosophy of Machiavelli seemed to cut politics free from its traditional link with morality by permitting to statesmen any means that secured the desired end. And the religious movements we know collectively as the Reformation broke with the Church of Rome and set the individual conscience, not ecclesiastical authority, at the centre of the religious life. Nothing, it seemed, was beyond questioning, nothing impossible.

Shakespeare's drama is innovative and challenging in exactly the way of the Renaissance. It examines and questions the beliefs, assumptions and politics upon which Elizabethan society was founded. And although the plays always conclude in a restoration of order and stability, many critics are inclined to argue that their imaginative energy goes into subverting, rather than reinforcing, traditional values. Frequently, figures of authority are undercut by some comic or parodic figure: against the Duke in *Measure for Measure* is set Lucio; against Prospero in *The Tempest*, Caliban; against Henry IV, Falstaff. Despairing, critical, dissident, disillusioned, unbalanced, rebellious, mocking voices are repeatedly to be heard in the plays, rejecting, resenting, defying the established order. They belong always to marginal, socially unacceptable figures, 'licensed', as it were, by their situations to say what would be unacceptable from socially privileged or responsible citizens. The

CHECK THE NET

The Luminarium site has links to a wide range of historical information on sixteenth-century topics including astronomy, medicine, economics and technology: **http://www.luminarium.org**.

question is: are such characters given these views to discredit them, or were they the only ones through whom a voice could be given to radical and dissident ideas? Was Shakespeare a conservative or a revolutionary?

Renaissance culture was intensely nationalistic. With the break-up of the internationalism of the Middle Ages the evolving nation states which still mark the map of Europe began for the first time to acquire distinctive cultural identities. There was intense rivalry among them as they sought to achieve, in their own vernacular languages, a culture that could equal that of Greece and Rome. Spenser's great allegorical epic poem *The Faerie Queene*, which began to appear from 1590, celebrated Elizabeth and was intended to outdo the poetic achievements of France and Italy and to stand beside the works of Virgil and Homer. Shakespeare is equally preoccupied with national identity. His history plays tell an epic story that examines how modern England came into being through the conflicts of the fifteenth-century Wars of the Roses which brought the Tudors to the throne. He is fascinated, too, by the related subject of politics and the exercise of power. With the collapse of medieval feudalism and the authority of local barons, the royal court in the Renaissance came to assume a new status as the centre of power and patronage. It was here that the destiny of a country was shaped. Courts, and how to succeed in them, consequently fascinated the Renaissance; and they fascinated Shakespeare and his audience.

CHECK THE BOOK

Benedict Anderson's book on the rise of the nation and nationalism, *Imagined Communities* (revised edition 1991), has been influential for its definition of the nation as 'an imagined political community' – imagined in part through cultural productions such as Shakespeare's history plays.

But the dramatic gaze is not merely admiring; through a variety of devices, a critical perspective is brought to bear. The court may be paralleled by a very different world, revealing uncomfortable similarities (for example, Henry's court and the Boar's Head tavern, ruled over by Falstaff in *Henry IV*). Its hypocrisy may be bitterly denounced (for example, in the diatribes of the mad Lear) and its self-seeking ambition represented disturbingly in the figure of a Machiavellian villain (such as Edmund in *Lear*) or a malcontent (such as Iago in *Othello*). Shakespeare is fond of displacing the court to another context, the better to examine its assumptions and pretensions and to offer alternatives to the courtly life (for example, in the pastoral setting of the forest of Arden in *As You Like It* or

Prospero's island in *The Tempest*). Courtiers are frequently figures of fun whose unmanly sophistication ('neat and trimly dressed, / Fresh as a bridegroom ... perfumed like a milliner', says Hotspur of such a man in *1 Henry IV*, I.3.33–6) is contrasted with plain-speaking integrity: Oswald is set against Kent in *King Lear*.

When thinking of these matters, we should remember that stage plays were subject to censorship, and any criticism had therefore to be muted or oblique: direct criticism of the monarch or contemporary English court would not be tolerated. This has something to do with why Shakespeare's plays are always set either in the past, or abroad.

CHECK THE FILM

We can get a modern equivalent of the effect of this displacement from Christine Edzard's film of *As You Like It* (1992). Here, the court scenes are set in the luxurious headquarters of a bank or company; the woodland scenes amid a sort of 'cardboard city' of social outcasts and the vulnerable.

The nationalism of the English Renaissance was reinforced by Protestantism. Henry VIII had broken with Rome in the 1530s and in Shakespeare's time there was an independent Protestant state church. Because the Pope in Rome had excommunicated Queen Elizabeth as a heretic and relieved the English of their allegiance to the crown, there was deep suspicion of Roman Catholics as potential traitors. This was enforced by the attempted invasion of the Spanish Armada in 1588. This was a religiously inspired crusade to overthrow Elizabeth and restore England to Roman Catholic allegiance. Roman Catholicism was hence easily identified with hostility to England. Its association with disloyalty and treachery was then reinforced by the Gunpowder Plot of 1605, a Roman Catholic attempt to destroy the government of England.

Shakespeare's plays are remarkably free from direct religious sentiment, but their emphases are Protestant. Young women, for example, are destined for marriage, not for nunneries (precisely what Isabella appears to escape at the end of *Measure for Measure*); friars are dubious characters, full of schemes and deceptions, if with benign intentions, as in *Much Ado About Nothing* or *Romeo and Juliet*. (We should add that Puritans, extreme Protestants, are even less kindly treated than Roman Catholics: for example, Malvolio in *Twelfth Night*).

The central figures of the plays are frequently individuals beset by temptation, by the lure of evil – Angelo in *Measure for Measure*,

Othello, Lear, Macbeth – and not only in tragedies: Falstaff is described as 'that old white-bearded Satan' (*1 Henry IV*, II.4.454). We follow their inner struggles. Shakespeare's heroes have the preoccupation with self and the introspective tendencies encouraged by Protestantism: his tragic heroes are haunted by their consciences, seeking their true selves, agonising over what course of action to take as they follow what can often be understood as a kind of spiritual progress towards heaven or hell.

SHAKESPEARE'S THEATRE

The theatre for which the plays were written was one of the most remarkable innovations of the Renaissance. There had been no theatres or acting companies during the medieval period. Performed on carts and in open spaces at Christian festivals, plays had been almost exclusively religious. Such professional actors as there were wandered the country putting on a variety of entertainments in the yards of inns, on makeshift stages in market squares, or anywhere else suitable. They did not perform full-length plays, but mimes, juggling and comedy acts. Such actors were regarded by officialdom and polite society as little better than vagabonds and layabouts.

Just before Shakespeare went to London all this began to change. A number of young men who had been to the universities of Oxford and Cambridge came to London in the 1580s and began to write plays that made use of what they had learned about the classical drama of ancient Greece and Rome. Plays such as John Lyly's *Alexander and Campaspe* (1584), Christopher Marlowe's *Tamburlaine the Great* (about 1587) and Thomas Kyd's *The Spanish Tragedy* (1588–9) were unlike anything that had been written in English before. They were full-length plays on secular subjects, taking their plots from history and legend, adopting many of the devices of Classical drama, and offering a range of characterisation and situation hitherto unattempted in English drama. With the exception of Lyly's prose dramas, they were composed in the unrhymed iambic pentameters (blank verse), which the Earl of Surrey had introduced into English earlier in the sixteenth century. This was a freer and more expressive medium than the rhymed verse

CHECK THE NET

Find out more about the Shakespearean theatre at **www.reading.ac. uk/globe**. This web site describes the historical researches undertaken in connection with the Globe theatre on London's Bankside, which was rebuilt in the late 1990s.

THE GLOBE THEATRE,

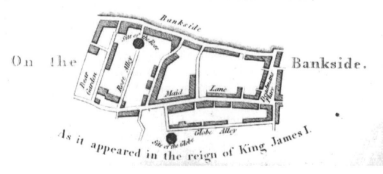

On the Bankside.

As it appeared in the reign of King James I.

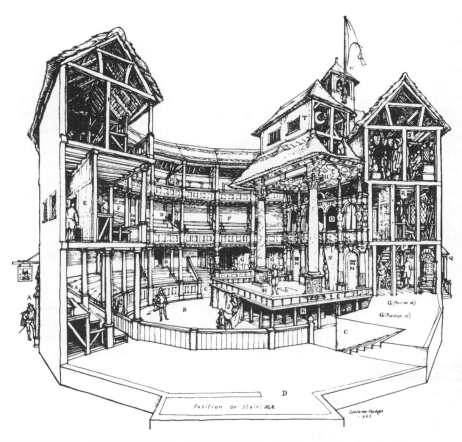

A CONJECTURAL RECONSTRUCTION OF THE INTERIOR OF THE GLOBE PLAYHOUSE

AA Main entrance
B The Yard
CC Entrances to lowest galleries
D Entrance to staircase and upper galleries
E Corridor serving the different sections of the middle gallery
F Middle gallery ('Twopenny Rooms')
G 'Gentlemen's Rooms or Lords Rooms'
H The stage
J The hanging being put up round the stage
K The 'Hell' under the stage
L The stage trap, leading down to the Hell
MM Stage doors

N Curtained 'place behind the stage'
O Gallery above the stage, used as required sometimes by musicians, sometimes by spectators, and often as part of the play
P Back-stage area (the tiring-house)
Q Tiring-house door
R Dressing-rooms
S Wardrobe and storage
T The hut housing the machine for lowering enthroned gods, etc., to the stage
U The 'Heavens'
W Hoisting the playhouse flag

CHECK THE BOOK

The most authoritative book on what we know about the theatre of Shakespeare's time is Andrew Gurr's *The Shakespearean Stage* (CUP, 1992).

CONTEXT

Whereas now we would conceptualise a visit to the theatre as going to *see* a play, the most common Elizabethan phrase was 'to go *hear* a play' (as in *The Taming of the Shrew*, Induction 2.130) – thus registering the different sensory priorities of the early modern theatre.

of medieval drama. It was the drama of these 'university wits' that Shakespeare challenged when he came to London. Greene was one of them, and we have heard how little he liked Shakespeare setting himself up as a dramatist.

The most significant change of all, however, was that these dramatists wrote for the professional theatre. In 1576 James Burbage built the first permanent theatre in England, in Shoreditch, just beyond London's northern boundary. It was called simply 'The Theatre'. Others soon followed. Thus, when Shakespeare came to London, there was a flourishing drama, theatres and companies of actors waiting for him, such as there had never been before in England. His company performed at James Burbage's Theatre until 1596, and used the Swan and Curtain until they moved into their own new theatre, the Globe, in 1599. It was burned down in 1613 when a cannon was fired during a performance of Shakespeare's *Henry VIII*.

With the completion in 1996 of Sam Wanamaker's project to construct in London a replica of the Globe, and with productions now running there, a version of Shakespeare's theatre can be experienced at first hand. It is very different to the usual modern experience of drama. The form of the Elizabethan theatre derived from the inn yards and animal baiting rings in which actors had been accustomed to perform in the past. They were circular wooden buildings with a paved courtyard in the middle open to the sky. A rectangular stage jutted out into the middle of this yard. Some of the audience stood in the yard (or 'pit') to watch the play. They were thus on three sides of the stage, close up to it and on a level with it. These 'groundlings' paid only a penny to get in, but for wealthier spectators there were seats in three covered tiers or galleries between the inner and outer walls of the building, extending round most of the auditorium and overlooking the pit and the stage. Such a theatre could hold about 3,000 spectators. The yards were about 24m in diameter and the rectangular stage approximately 12 by 9m and 1.67m high. Shakespeare aptly called such a theatre a 'wooden O' in the prologue to *Henry V* (line 13).

The stage itself was partially covered by a roof or canopy, which projected from the wall at the rear of the stage and was supported by two posts at the front. This protected the stage and performers from inclement weather, and to it were secured winches and other machinery for stage effects. On either side at the back of the stage was a door. These led into the dressing room (or 'tiring house') and it was by means of these doors that actors entered and left the stage. Between these doors was a small recess or alcove which was curtained off. Such a 'discovery place' served, for example, for Juliet's bedroom when in Act IV Scene 4 of *Romeo and Juliet* the Nurse went to the back of the stage and drew the curtain to find Juliet apparently dead on her bed. Above the discovery place was a balcony, used for the famous balcony scenes of *Romeo and Juliet* (II.2 and III.5), or for the battlements of Richard's castle when he is confronted by Bolingbroke in *Richard II* (III.3). Actors (all parts in the Elizabethan theatre were taken by boys or men) had access to the area beneath the stage; from here, in the 'cellarage', would have come the voice of the ghost of Hamlet's father (*Hamlet*, II.1.150–82).

On these stages there was very little in the way of scenery or props – there was nowhere to store them (there were no wings in this theatre) nor any way to set them up (no tabs across the stage), and, anyway, productions had to be transportable for performance at court or at noble houses. The stage was bare, which is why characters often tell us where they are: there was nothing on the stage to indicate location. It is also why location is so rarely topographical, and much more often symbolic. It suggests a dramatic mood or situation, rather than a place: Lear's barren heath reflects his destitute state, as the storm his emotional turmoil.

None of the plays printed in Shakespeare's lifetime marks Act or scene divisions. These have been introduced by later editors, but they should not mislead us into supposing that there was any break in Elizabethan performances such as might happen today while the curtains are closed and the set is changed. The staging of Elizabethan plays was continuous, with the many short 'scenes' of which Shakespeare's plays are often constructed following one after another in quick succession. We have to think of a more fluid, and much faster production than we are generally used to: in the prologues to *Romeo and Juliet* (line 12) and *Henry VIII* (line 13)

CONTEXT

We do not know much about the props list for a theatre company in Shakespeare's time, although the evidence we do have suggests that there were some quite ambitious examples: one list dating from 1598 includes decorated cloths depicting cities or the night sky, items of armour, horses' heads and 'one hell mouth', probably for performances of Marlowe's famous play *Doctor Faustus*.

Shakespeare speaks of the playing time as only two hours. It is because plays were staged continuously that exits and entrances are written in as part of the script: characters speak as they enter or leave the stage because otherwise there would be a silence while, in full view, they took up their positions. (This is also why dead bodies have to be carried off: they cannot get up and walk off.)

In 1608 Shakespeare's company, the King's Men, acquired the Blackfriars Theatre, a smaller, rectangular indoor theatre, holding about 700 people, with seats for all the members of the audience, facilities for elaborate stage effects and, because it was enclosed, artificial lighting. It has been suggested that the plays written for this 'private' theatre differed from those written for the Globe, since, as it cost more to go to a private theatre, the audience came from a higher social stratum and demanded the more elaborate and courtly entertainment which Shakespeare's romances provide. However, the King's Men continued to play at the Globe in the summer, using Blackfriars in the winter, and it is not certain that Shakespeare's last plays were written specifically for the Blackfriars theatre, or first performed there.

READING SHAKESPEARE

Shakespeare's plays were written for this stage, but there is also a sense in which they were written *by* the stage. The material and physical circumstances of their production in such theatres had a profound effect upon the nature of Elizabethan plays. Unless we bear this in mind, we are likely to find them very strange, for we will read with expectations shaped by our own familiarity with modern fiction and modern drama which is, by and large, realistic; it seeks to persuade us that what we are reading or watching is really happening. This is quite foreign to Shakespeare. If we try to read him like this, we shall find ourselves irritated by the improbabilities of his plot, confused by his chronology, puzzled by locations, frustrated by unanswered questions and dissatisfied by the motivation of the action. The absurd ease with which disguised persons pass through Shakespeare's plays is a case in point: why does no one recognise people they know so well? There is a great deal of psychological accuracy in Shakespeare's plays, but we are far from any attempt at realism.

CHECK THE BOOK
Deborah Cartmell's *Interpreting Shakespeare on Screen* (2000) is recommended for its clear and interesting sense of the possibilities and the requirements of approaching Shakespeare through the cinema.

The reason is that in Shakespeare's theatre it was impossible to pretend that the audience was not watching a contrived performance. In a modern theatre, the audience is encouraged to forget itself as it becomes absorbed by the action on stage. The worlds of the spectators and of the actors are sharply distinguished by the lighting: in the dark auditorium the audience is passive, silent, anonymous, receptive and attentive; on the lighted stage the actors are active, vocal, demonstrative and dramatic. (The distinction is, of course, still more marked in the cinema.) There is no communication between the two worlds: for the audience to speak would be interruptive; for the actors to address the audience would be to break the illusion of the play. In the Elizabethan theatre, this distinction did not exist, and for two reasons: first, performances took place in the open air and in daylight which illuminated everyone equally; secondly, the spectators were all around the stage (and wealthier spectators actually on it), and were dressed no differently from the actors, who wore contemporary dress. In such a theatre, spectators would be as aware of each other as of the actors; they could not lose their identity in a corporate group, nor could they ever forget that they were spectators at a performance. There was no chance that they could believe 'this is really happening'.

This, then, was communal theatre, not only in the sense that it was going on in the middle of a crowd but also in the sense that the crowd joined in. Elizabethan audiences had none of our deference: they did not keep quiet, nor arrive on time, nor remain for the whole performance. They joined in, interrupted, even getting on the stage. And plays were preceded and followed by jigs and clowning. It was all much more like our experience of a pantomime, and at a pantomime we are fully aware, and are meant to be aware, that we are watching games being played with reality. The conventions of pantomime revel in their own artificiality: the fishnet tights are to signal that the handsome prince is a woman, the Dame's monstrous false breasts signal that 'she' is a man.

Something very similar is the case with Elizabethan theatre: it utilised its very theatricality. Instead of trying to persuade spectators that they are not in a theatre watching a performance,

CONTEXT

The Romantic critic Samuel Taylor Coleridge argued that literature requires our 'willing suspension of disbelief': but it is not clear that the theatre of the Shakespearean period did require its audience to forget that they were in a theatre. Certainly, remarks calling attention to the theatrical setting are commonplace – in comedies such as *Twelfth Night* (III.4.125) and *As You Like It* (II.7.139–43), and in tragedies including *Macbeth* (V.5.23–5) – making it more difficult to forget the theatricality of the stories depicted.

Elizabethan plays acknowledge the presence of the audience. It is addressed not only by prologues, epilogues and choruses, but also in soliloquies. There is no realistic reason why characters should suddenly explain themselves to empty rooms, but, of course, there is no empty room. The actor is surrounded by people. Soliloquies are not addressed to the world of the play; they are for the audience's benefit. And that audience's complicity is assumed: when a character like Prospero declares himself to be invisible, it is accepted that he is. Disguises are taken to be impenetrable, however improbable, and we are to accept impossibly contrived situations, such as barely hidden characters remaining undetected (indeed, on the Elizabethan stage there was nowhere at all they could hide).

CHECK THE NET

Search the 'Designing Shakespeare' database at PADS **(www.pads.ahds. ac.uk)** for an extensive collection of photographs from different productions available online.

These, then, are plays that are aware of themselves as dramas; in critical terminology, they are self-reflexive, commenting upon themselves as dramatic pieces and prompting the audience to think about the theatrical experience. They do this not only through their direct address to the audience but also through their fondness for the play-within-a-play (which reminds the audience that the encompassing play is also a play) and their constant use of images from, and allusions to, the theatre. They are fascinated by role-playing, by acting, appearance and reality. Things are rarely what they seem, either in comedy (for example, in *A Midsummer Night's Dream*) or tragedy (*Romeo and Juliet*). This offers one way to think about those disguises: they are thematic rather than realistic. Kent's disguise in *Lear* reveals his true, loyal self, while Edmund, who is not disguised, hides his true self. In *As You Like It*, Rosalind is more truly herself disguised as a man than when dressed as a woman.

The effect of all this is to confuse the distinction we would make between 'real life' and 'acting'. The case of Rosalind, for example, raises searching questions about gender roles, about how far it is 'natural' to be womanly or manly: how does the stage, on which a man can play a woman playing a man (and have a man fall in love with him/her), differ from life, in which we assume the roles we think appropriate to masculine and feminine behaviour? The same is true of political roles: when a Richard II or Lear is so aware of the regal part he is performing, of the trappings and rituals of kingship, their plays raise the uncomfortable possibility that the answer to the question of what constitutes a successful king is simply: a good actor. Indeed, human life generally is repeatedly rendered through the imagery of the stage, from Macbeth's 'Life's but a walking shadow, a poor player / That struts and frets his hour upon the stage / And then is heard no more' (V.5.23–5) to Prospero's paralleling of human life to a performance which, like the globe (both world and theatre!) will end (IV.I.146–58). When life is a fiction, like this play, or this play is a fiction like life, what is the difference? 'All the world's a stage...' (*As You Like It*, II.7.139).

LITERARY BACKGROUND

SOURCES

Although a wide range of literature dealing with calumny against an innocent woman like Hero was available to Shakespeare, he drew for the main plot of *Much Ado* principally upon three romances. The primary source was the twenty-second story of Matteo Bandello's collection of *Novelle* printed in Lucca in 1554 and translated into French and expanded by Belleforest in *Histoires Tragiques* in 1569. Shakespeare roughly adopted the characters of Leonato, Don Pedro and Hero from this source. However, unlike the poor Leonato of the source, Shakespeare's is a rich governor, which makes the insult of his calumny to a near equal's daughter the more offensive.

In Bandello's tale, Sir Timbreo (Claudio's prototype) falls in love with Fenicia, daughter of Lionato di Lionati, a gentleman of Messina. Another knight, Girondo, watches their betrothal with jealous fury and then bribes a young man to trick Timbreo into believing that she was unfaithful. Timbreo, thinking that he had witnessed a gallant climbing into her bed chamber, writes a message to Lionato breaking off the engagement and denouncing Fenicia. Lionato, doubting her guilt, ascribes the breaking of the match to his poverty. Fenicia falls into a coma with grief, though not before wishing Timbreo happiness and declaring her own innocence. Upon her recovery, her father hides her away and at her 'funeral' has a dirge sung proclaiming her innocence. Girondo, afflicted by remorse, offers his sword and confesses his plot to Timbreo at Fenicia's tomb. Too remorseful for revenge, he and Girondo go to

> **CONTEXT**
>
> The poet Walter Raleigh wrote a poem on this image of life as theatre, which begins 'What is our life? A play of passion', in which 'Our mothers' wombs the tiring houses be, / Where we are dressed for this short comedy'. There's a twist at the end of the short verse: 'Only we die in earnest, that's no jest.'

Lionato who imposes a light penalty that they should marry according to his choice. After a year Timbreo is presented to a gracefully matured Fenicia under the name of Lucilla. Her sister, Belfiore, is bestowed upon Girondo; a double marriage is celebrated and Lionato is honoured by the king, who presents both daughters with handsome dowries.

CONTEXT

Orlando furioso, Ariosto's poem, first published in 1531, was designed as a sequel to Boiardo's poem, *Orlando innamorato* of 1487 on the subject of falling in love.

Another, minor source is the fifth book of Ariosto's *Orlando furioso*, translated by Harington in 1591. It has the impersonation of a heroine, Genevra, by a maid, Dalinda, mistress of the villain, to alienate the lady's lover. Although the part of Margaret comes from Ariosto, Dalinda admits a man to her room, as Margaret does not, which enables Shakespeare to preserve her ambiguous innocence until the end.

The story of Phedon and Philemon in the second book of Edmund Spenser's *The Faerie Queene* constitutes the other significant source. Phedon was about to marry Lady Claribel when Philemon, with whom he had grown up, reported her unfaithful with a groom of low degree, like Borachio. Philemon had seduced Claribel's maid whom he had talked into dressing in her mistress's clothes for an assignation with the groom, witnessed by Phedon. He killed Claribel, after which her maid revealed her part in the deception, whereupon he poisoned Philemon and was pursuing the maid when met by Sir Guyon.

Although no specific source has been found for the Watch or the sparring lovers, Beatrice and Benedick, Castiglione's *Il Cortegiano* (The Courtier) provided a model of courtly conversation, where wit and mockery could be maintained in a good-humoured battle of the sexes. There is strong evidence from John Aubrey's *Brief Lives* that the Watch were taken from life.

HISTORICAL BACKGROUND

MESSINA

Messina is a port in north-eastern Sicily separated from Calabria by the narrow straits of Messina. This setting gave credence to the conventions of chastity and chivalry. Beatrice's 'Kill Claudio!' (IV.1.279) for the slander of Hero was passionately meant and endorsed by it.

Shakespeare took the setting of Messina from his sources, and although it can be argued that love and honour are universal concerns, as the productions mentioned above suggest, Shakespeare does give them a local flavour, however. Claudio comes from Florence, Benedick from Padua and Don Pedro is a prince of Aragon.

The House of Aragon had ruled Sicily from the end of the thirteenth century, and Sicily would continue to be under Spanish control throughout the seventeenth, a rigid control which undermined the influence of the old privileged classes, and kept it a backward, feudalised society. Unlike some of the other Italian city-states, here the role of the *podestà* or governor had been weakened. Here Leonato is presented as the somewhat humble governor of Messina, in contrast to Don Pedro's arrogance, and Shakespeare **satirises** the vanity of the aristocracy of this influential European state.

Messina is presented as a domesticated city-state, a haven from war. Its warmth and cultivation are suggested through references to oranges and gardens. There is a languid melancholy in the pivotal song of Balthasar, 'Sigh no more' (II.3.53) which also underlines the strict code of male honour and the subordination of women. Literature indicates that the Elizabethan stereotype of the Italian was pejorative – scheming, cowardly, underhand and temperamental.

Messina's rigid formality is represented in the masked ball, which also underlines the importance of appearances and the tendency to deceit. The climate is of distrust, with constant spying of one faction upon another. It is extremely patriarchal, with Leonato assuming the right to dispose of Hero to whomsoever he wishes and to disown her when she is merely seen to have dishonoured him. The double standard is stressed through references to Benedick's behaviour as a libertine in Venice, with Claudio as his boon

CHECK THE FILM

An Italianate setting was used in Kenneth Branagh's 1993 film of *Much Ado*, while Franco Zeffirelli's 1965 production was more specifically turn-of-the-century Sicilian with a Mediterranean setting and a mafioso Don John in a double-breasted suit.

companion. Don Pedro represents the Spanish ruling class, with constant pomposity and insistence upon his superior status.

If the hot-headedness of the Italian is implied in the speed with which Hero is condemned rashly on such shallow evidence, the more positive spontaneity of the society is implied in the wit of Beatrice and Benedick, the warmth of the song and the sometimes melodramatic alternation of mood. Messina thus enabled Shakespeare to feel confident of his audience's distance from that society and to dramatise attitudes and emotions more starkly enacted than in his native England.

World events	Shakespeare's life *(dates for plays are approximate)*	Literature/drama
1282 Peter III of Aragon invited to become king of Sicily		
1442 Alfonso V the Magnanimous, Aragonese ruler of Sicily, wins control of the Kingdom of Naples		
1458 On Alfonso's death, Aragon and Sicily go to his brother John; the Kingdom of Naples to his legitimised bastard son, Ferrante, who proves himself treacherous and cruel		
1492 Columbus sets sails for America		
		1513 Niccolò Machiavelli, *The Prince*
		1528 Castiglione, *Book of the Courtier*
		1532 Ariosto, *Orlando Furioso* (source)
1534 Henry VIII breaks with Rome		
		1554 Matteo Bandelli, *Novelle* (source)
1556 Archbishop Cranmer burnt at stake		
1558 Elizabeth I accedes to throne		
		1562 Lope de Vega, great Spanish dramatist, born
	1564 (26 April) **William Shakespeare** baptised Stratford-upon-Avon (birth traditionally dated 23 April, St George's Day	
		1569 Belleforest, *Histoires Tragiques* (source)
1570 Elizabeth I excommunicated by Pope Pius V		
	1576 James Burbage builds the first theatre in England, at Shoreditch	
1577 Francis Drake sets out on voyage round the world		

World events	Shakespeare's life *(dates for plays are approximate)*	Literature/drama
		1580 (c.) Sir Philip Sidney, *An Apologie for Poetrie*
	1582 Shakespeare marries Anne Hathaway	
	1583 Their daughter, Susanna, is born	
1584 Raleigh's sailors land in Virginia		
	1585 Their twins, Hamnet and Judith, born	
	LATE 1580s – EARLY 90s Probably writes *Henry VI (Parts I, II, III)* and *Richard III*	
1587 Execution of Mary Queen of Scots		
1588 The Spanish Armada defeated		**1588–9** Thomas Kyd, *The Spanish Tragedy*
		1590 Edmund Spenser, *Faerie Queene* (Books I-III) (source)
1592 Plague in London closes theatres	**1592** Recorded as being a London actor and an 'upstart crow'	**1592** Christopher Marlowe, *Dr Faustus*
	1592–4 Writes *Comedy of Errors*	
		1593 Christopher Marlowe killed in tavern brawl
	1594 ONWARDS Writes exclusively for the Lord Chamberlain's Men	
	1595 (PRE-) *Two Gentlemen of Verona*, *The Taming of the Shrew* and *Love's Labour's Lost* probably written.	**1595** Death of William Painter, whose *Palace of Pleasure* provided sources for plots of many Elizabethan dramas
	1595 (C.) *Romeo and Juliet* and *A Midsummer Night's Dream*	
1596 English raid on Cadiz	**1596–8** First performance, *The Merchant of Venice*	**1596** Edmund Spenser, *Faerie Queene* (Books IV-VI)
	1598–9 Globe Theatre built at Southwark; probably writes *Much Ado About Nothing*	**1598** Ben Jonson, *Every Man in his Humour*

World events	Shakespeare's life *(dates for plays are approximate)*	Literature/drama
		1599 Ben Jonson, *Every Man out of his Humour*
	1600 *A Midsummer Night's Dream*, **Much Ado About Nothing** and *The Merchant of Venice* printed in quartos	
	1600–1 *Hamlet*	
	1600–2 *Twelfth Night* written	
1603 Death of Queen Elizabeth Tudor; accession of James Stuart	**1603 ONWARDS** His company enjoys patronage of James I as the King's Men	
	1604 *Othello* performed	
1605 Discovery of Guy Fawkes's plot	**1605** First version of *King Lear*	**1605** Cervantes, *Don Quijote de la Mancha*
	1606 *Macbeth*	**1606** Ben Jonson, *Volpone;* Michael Drayton, *Odes*
	1606–7 *Antony and Cleopatra*	
	1608 The King's Men acquire Blackfriars Theatre for winter performances	
		1609 Ben Jonson, *Epicoene, or The Silent Woman*
1610 William Harvey discovers circulation of blood		**1610** Ben Jonson, *The Alchemist*
	1611 *Cymbeline, The Winter's Tale* and *The Tempest* performed	**1611** 'King James' Bible (authorised version)
1612 Last burning of heretics in England		
	1613 Globe Theatre burns down	
		1614 Sir Walter Raleigh, *The History of the World*
	1616 Death of William Shakespeare (23 April)	
1618 Raleigh executed for treason; Thirty Years War begins in Europe		
		1622 Birth of French dramatist Molière
	1623 First folio of Shakespeare's works	

FURTHER READING

Harold Bloom, ed., *William Shakespeare's Much Ado About Nothing: Modern Critical Interpretations*, Chelsea House, 1988
> A thought-provoking collection of contemporary critical essays examining the play from various theoretical perspectives – social, historical, psychoanalytical, sexual, political

John Russell Brown, ed., *Much Ado About Nothing and As You Like It:: A Casebook*, Macmillan, 1979
> A collection of essays

Deborah Cartmell, *Shakespeare on Screen*, Palgrove, 2000
> Approaches Shakespeare through film

Cookson & Loughrey, eds, *Much Ado About Nothing*, Longman Critical Essays, 1989
> Various critical perspectives are adopted in essays aimed at A-level students, which encourage close reading of the text with a focus on central characters and themes

John Cox, ed., *Much Ado About Nothing: Shakespeare in Production*, Cambridge University Press, 1997
> Exhaustive survey of dramatic interpretations of the play together with a text annotated with notable interpretations of specific speeches. The text is brought to life as a play and opened to interpretation

Walter Davis, ed., *Twentieth Century Interpretations of Much Ado About Nothing*, Prentice-Hall, 1969
> A sound and varied collection of essays on the play upon which Bloom's collection builds

Andrew Gurr, *The Shakespearean Stage, 1574–1642*, 3rd edn, Cambridge University Press, 1992
> The most authoritative book about the theatre in Shakespeare's time

Pamela Mason, *Much Ado About Nothing: Text and Performance*, Macmillan, 1992
> The first half of the book is a critical examination of key scenes, the second half an account of five significant productions. The two halves are complementary and the book admirably concise and illuminating

J.R. Mulryne, *Shakespeare: Much Ado About Nothing*, Edward Arnold, 1965
> Detailed analysis of the play scene by scene; particularly useful as a preliminary aid to understanding and for revision

Roger Sales, *Much Ado About Nothing*, Penguin Critical Studies, 1987
> Highly original individual interpretation of the play which makes excellent use of historical research and offers special insight into the male characters and honour

S. Schoenbaum, *William Shakespeare:: A Compact Documentary Life*, Clarendon Press, 1977
> The most authoritative biography

LITERARY TERMS

allegory a story or situation written in such a way as to have two distinct coherent meanings

alliteration a series of repeated consonants in a stretch of language, usually at the beginning of words or stressed syllables

antithesis the opposition of contrasting ideas in neighbouring sentences or clauses, using opposite or contrasting forms of words

aphorism a generally accepted truth or principle expressed in a short, pithy way

bathos a ludicrous descent from the elevated treatment of a subject to the ordinary or dull

blank verse unrhymed **iambic pentameter**

epigram any short poem which has a sharp turn of thought or point; now used of witty sayings in general

euphemism a word or phrase that is less blunt than the original unpleasant, embarrassing or frightening one

euphuism a kind of prose writing which is exaggeratedly elaborate, full of **antithesis, alliteration**, ornate **similes** and learned allusions. Popular in the late sixteenth century

hyperbole emphasis by exaggeration

iambic pentameter a line of poetry consisting of five iambic feet (iambic consisting of a weak syllable followed by a strong one)

irony covert sarcasm; saying one thing while meaning another; using words to convey the opposite of their literal meaning; saying something that has one meaning for someone knowledgeable about a situation and another meaning for those who are not; incongruity between what might be expected and what actually happens; ill-timed arrival of an event which has been hoped for. **Dramatic irony** occurs when the development of the plot allows the audience to possess more information about what is happening than some of the characters themselves have. Characters may also speak in a dramatically ironic way, saying something that points to events to come without understanding the significance of their words

malapropism using the wrong word, often with a similar sound. From Mrs Malaprop in Sheridan's *The Rivals*, 1755

metaphor a figure of speech in which a descriptive term, or name or action characteristic of one object is applied to another to suggest a likeness between them, but which does not use 'like' or 'as' in comparison

oxymoron a special variety of **paradox**; a figure of speech in which contradictory terms are brought together in what might at first seem an impossible combination paradox a statement which seems self-contradictory, unbelievable or absurd, yet which contains a truth

pathos moments which provoke strong feelings of pity and sorrow

personification a variety of figurative language in which things or ideas are treated as if they were human beings, with human attributes and feelings

quibble in the context of this play, a pun

satire literature which examines vice or folly and makes them appear ridiculous or contemptible

simile a figure of speech containing a comparison of two things and using the word 'like' or 'as'

soliloquy a dramatic convention which allow a character to speak directly to the audience as if thinking aloud about motives, feelings and decisions

synonym a word with a meaning identical to that of another word

Educated at universities in Canada, and Cambridge and Sussex Universities, Ross Stuart has lectured at Queen's University, and the University of New Brunswick, and for four years was a senior lecturer in English at the University of Fes in Morocco. He currently teaches English at Christ's Hospital School in Horsham and has published articles on English fiction and autobiography and on Canadian poetry.

General editor

Martin Gray, former Head of the Department of English Studies at the University of Stirling, and of Literary Studies at the University of Luton

Maya Angelou
I Know Why the Caged Bird Sings

Jane Austen
Pride and Prejudice

Alan Ayckbourn
Absent Friends

Elizabeth Barrett Browning
Selected Poems

Robert Bolt
A Man for All Seasons

Harold Brighouse
Hobson's Choice

Charlotte Brontë
Jane Eyre

Emily Brontë
Wuthering Heights

Shelagh Delaney
A Taste of Honey

Charles Dickens
David Copperfield
Great Expectations
Hard Times
Oliver Twist

Roddy Doyle
Paddy Clarke Ha Ha Ha

George Eliot
Silas Marner
The Mill on the Floss

Anne Frank
The Diary of a Young Girl

William Golding
Lord of the Flies

Oliver Goldsmith
She Stoops to Conquer

Willis Hall
The Long and the Short and the Tall

Thomas Hardy
Far from the Madding Crowd
The Mayor of Casterbridge
Tess of the d'Urbervilles
The Withered Arm and other Wessex Tales

L.P. Hartley
The Go-Between

Seamus Heaney
Selected Poems

Susan Hill
I'm the King of the Castle

Barry Hines
A Kestrel for a Knave

Louise Lawrence
Children of the Dust

Harper Lee
To Kill a Mockingbird

Laurie Lee
Cider with Rosie

Arthur Miller
The Crucible
A View from the Bridge

Robert O'Brien
Z for Zachariah

Frank O'Connor
My Oedipus Complex and Other Stories

George Orwell
Animal Farm

J.B. Priestley
An Inspector Calls
When We Are Married

Willy Russell
Educating Rita
Our Day Out

J.D. Salinger
The Catcher in the Rye

William Shakespeare
Henry IV Part I
Henry V
Julius Caesar
Macbeth
The Merchant of Venice
A Midsummer Night's Dream
Much Ado About Nothing

Romeo and Juliet
The Tempest
Twelfth Night

George Bernard Shaw
Pygmalion

Mary Shelley
Frankenstein

R.C. Sherriff
Journey's End

Rukshana Smith
Salt on the snow

John Steinbeck
Of Mice and Men

Robert Louis Stevenson
Dr Jekyll and Mr Hyde

Jonathan Swift
Gulliver's Travels

Robert Swindells
Daz 4 Zoe

Mildred D. Taylor
Roll of Thunder, Hear My Cry

Mark Twain
Huckleberry Finn

James Watson
Talking in Whispers

Edith Wharton
Ethan Frome

William Wordsworth
Selected Poems

A Choice of Poets

Mystery Stories of the Nineteenth Century including The Signalman

Nineteenth Century Short Stories

Poetry of the First World War

Six Women Poets

For the AQA Anthology:

Duffy and Armitage & Pre-1914 Poetry

Heaney and Clarke & Pre-1914 Poetry

Poems from Different Cultures

Margaret Atwood
Cat's Eye
The Handmaid's Tale

Jane Austen
Emma
Mansfield Park
Persuasion
Pride and Prejudice
Sense and Sensibility

Alan Bennett
Talking Heads

William Blake
Songs of Innocence and of Experience

Charlotte Brontë
Jane Eyre
Villette

Emily Brontë
Wuthering Heights

Angela Carter
Nights at the Circus

Geoffrey Chaucer
The Franklin's Prologue and Tale
The Merchant's Prologue and Tale
The Miller's Prologue and Tale
The Prologue to the Canterbury Tales
The Wife of Bath's Prologue and Tale

Samuel Coleridge
Selected Poems

Joseph Conrad
Heart of Darkness

Daniel Defoe
Moll Flanders

Charles Dickens
Bleak House
Great Expectations
Hard Times

Emily Dickinson
Selected Poems

John Donne
Selected Poems

Carol Ann Duffy
Selected Poems

George Eliot
Middlemarch
The Mill on the Floss

T.S. Eliot
Selected Poems
The Waste Land

F. Scott Fitzgerald
The Great Gatsby

E.M. Forster
A Passage to India

Brian Friel
Translations

Thomas Hardy
Jude the Obscure
The Mayor of Casterbridge
The Return of the Native
Selected Poems
Tess of the d'Urbervilles

Seamus Heaney
Selected Poems from 'Opened Ground'

Nathaniel Hawthorne
The Scarlet Letter

Homer
The Iliad
The Odyssey

Aldous Huxley
Brave New World

Kazuo Ishiguro
The Remains of the Day

Ben Jonson
The Alchemist

James Joyce
Dubliners

John Keats
Selected Poems

Philip Larkin
The Whitsun Weddings and Selected Poems

Christopher Marlowe
Doctor Faustus
Edward II

Arthur Miller
Death of a Salesman

John Milton
Paradise Lost Books I & II

Toni Morrison
Beloved

George Orwell
Nineteen Eighty-Four

Sylvia Plath
Selected Poems

Alexander Pope
Rape of the Lock & Selected Poems

William Shakespeare
Antony and Cleopatra
As You Like It
Hamlet
Henry IV Part I
King Lear
Macbeth
Measure for Measure
The Merchant of Venice
A Midsummer Night's Dream
Much Ado About Nothing
Othello
Richard II
Richard III
Romeo and Juliet
The Taming of the Shrew
The Tempest
Twelfth Night
The Winter's Tale

George Bernard Shaw
Saint Joan

Mary Shelley
Frankenstein

Jonathan Swift
Gulliver's Travels and A Modest Proposal

Alfred Tennyson
Selected Poems

Virgil
The Aeneid

Alice Walker
The Color Purple

Oscar Wilde
The Importance of Being Earnest

Tennessee Williams
A Streetcar Named Desire
The Glass Menagerie

Jeanette Winterson
Oranges Are Not the Only Fruit

John Webster
The Duchess of Malfi

Virginia Woolf
To the Lighthouse

William Wordsworth
The Prelude and Selected Poems

W.B. Yeats
Selected Poems

Metaphysical Poets